# WHERE WERE THE ARABS?

# Where Were the Arabs?

*by Dorothy Fuldheim*

THE WORLD PUBLISHING COMPANY
Cleveland and New York

The excerpt on pages 76 and 77 is reprinted
by permission of Schocken Books, Inc., from *In
the Heart of the Seas* by S. Y. Agnon, copyright
© 1947 by Schocken Books, Inc.


Published by The World Publishing Company
2231 West 110th Street, Cleveland, Ohio 44102
Published simultaneously in Canada by
Nelson, Foster & Scott Ltd.

*First Edition*

Library of Congress Catalog Card Number:
67–30970

Printed in the United States of America

To Donald Perris, a doughty warrior himself.

# Contents

# Foreword

When Egypt closed the Gulf of 'Aqaba and U Thant dismissed the United Nations' contingent in the Gaza Strip, it was obvious that the somber clouds of war were gathering.

I had covered the Palestinian war in 1948. I had been in Egypt and Israel in 1956, and I knew with prescience that the Arabs' encirclement of Israel left her no alternative but to fight. The world watched with horror, but not a voice was raised by any nation or government to aid Israel; her doom seemed imminent.

The blossoming summer flowers might well have become a funeral wreath for Israel. Egypt had chosen the hour, but it was Israel that chose the moment. And when the Israeli Air Force winged its way into the Egyptian skies and paralyzed the Arab world, I flew to Israel to cover this dramatic and unbelievable war.

I have covered many major news events, but never have I experienced the emotional impact of this Israeli victory. Its place in recorded history will be emblazoned with wonderment and awe. Those June days will remain a page of history illuminated with brilliant military strategy and quiet heroism.

David slew Goliath because he was adroit enough to force the giant to face the sun, thus blurring his vision; so the Israelis met the Arab giant with superior planning and thought.

I have tried to recapture the emotion of these few days. For in less than the number of days in which the Lord labored to create the world, the Arab armies lay supine and the bronzed, dusty Israeli army raised the flags of victory. I witnessed the birth of the new Jew, the victorious Jew.

To put into words, to communicate the impact of this victory and the sudden surge of freedom and the release from apprehension experienced by the Israelis is an almost impossible assignment but I knew that I had been witness to an event destined to become one of man's heroic epics, and I have endeavored to describe it.

D. F.

Cleveland, Ohio
September, 1967

*The Middle East, June 5, 1967—June 10, 1967. The territory occupied by Israeli forces (shaded area) includes Jerusalem and Jordan's West Bank (June 7), the Sinai Peninsula (June 8), and a portion of Syria (June 10).*

# WHERE WERE THE ARABS?

# ✿ ONE

# No Room Service

WHEN ACTUAL WARFARE broke out following the Egyptian announcement that the Arab world was determined to annihilate Israel and destroy every Israeli, I went to the head of the Cleveland television station where I work as a news analyst and told him "I want to go to Israel."

Donald Perris's answer was short and singularly vehement: "Nonsense! It's ridiculous!" and he turned on his heel and walked away. I followed him, saying: "Look, if you had been manager of a station when Octavian was attacking Cleopatra's fleet with his Roman galleys at Actium, would you have refused to allow your chief news analyst to cover the event? Well, this is exactly what is going to happen in Israel! It is too important to miss." This time he did not even deign to answer as he strode down the hall; his long legs enabled him to proceed much faster than I could, but I pursued him: *"I am going to cover this war!"*

"You certainly are not," he snapped. "I am not going to have it on my conscience if anything happens to you. You are neither cautious, prudent, nor a mere twenty years old!" I had to admit to myself that that combination really left me no argument, but I persisted. Every place the manager looked that day he saw me. When he did not see me in person he found on his desk notes reading *"I'm going to Israel."* At last in sheer exasperation he conceded, "Well, if we can find some strong escort to guard you, perhaps I will withdraw my objections."

"Why don't you get me a prize fighter—he'd be strong," I suggested, adding, "but of course he's got to be good-looking, too."

I then further amended my requirements. My position was growing stronger. "I won't go with a prize fighter if he is *merely* strong and good-looking. He has to be bright, too."

Someone wanted to know where I expected to locate a bright prize fighter.

"That's your problem," I responded airily. "I am willing to go without anyone. I don't need an escort."

Then I added another stipulation: "I won't go with him unless he is strong, good-looking, bright, and has a good name. I don't want to go running around Israel with just *anyone!"* Naturally I was thinking that this would make it completely impossible to obtain anyone who would be satisfactory to all parties and I could take off by myself. But I was reckoning without the resourcefulness of Perris, for at that point someone came up with the name of the famous ballplayer Al Rosen.

By then (with no disparagement of Al Rosen, who is

distinguished and good-looking as well as a famous athlete) I would have gone with the Devil rather than stay in Cleveland.

"I'd be delighted to have Mr. Rosen with me," I shouted, and started for the phone to begin arrangements before Perris could change his mind. The State Department agreed to validate my passport for Israel and Senator Stephen M. Young, the junior Senator from Ohio, and his staff were kind and helpful in expediting my request.

Two days later, after working around the clock preparing programs that could be shown while I was away, I left Cleveland on one of the hottest days of the year, so hot that the asphalt pavement of New York streets literally stuck to the soles of my shoes.

I hardly knew Al Rosen. I had met him briefly once or twice. He turned out to be a delightful companion who insisted that we be accompanied by armed guards throughout our trip. I met him in New York and dined with his parents; then on the evening of June 7 he and I boarded the plane, which was packed. The only activity of the youngster who sat directly behind me consisted of kicking the back of my seat. By two o'clock in the morning with no sleep, I was a wreck. I turned around and said to the child's mother in my most dulcet tones: "Madame, would you ask your son to stop kicking my seat?"

"You ask him," she replied. "I'm ready to throw him out the window."

Not really wishing to contribute to a midnight murder, I said nothing more and endured the kicking.

It was very late at night when we arrived in Tel Aviv —the plane was hours late; schedules were not yet regular and I was tired from the hot and crowded ride from New York, but not so weary that I failed to be thoroughly enchanted by the sight of a paratrooper, at least 6'2", with startlingly bright blue eyes, wearing a magnificent blond beard, standing in the airport at Tel Aviv. He wore a red beret and carried his swagger stick with great *élan*. I stood and stared at him: if the Israeli army was brave, it was also most assuredly beautiful. I turned to Al Rosen and whispered: "Buy him for me."

Not until half past one in the morning could we climb into the waiting car and begin the drive to Jerusalem. I was familiar with the terrain from previous trips and was interested to note that some of the tanks destroyed in the war of 1956 could still be seen rusting on the road; the Israeli government had left them there as mementos of that war. It is a hilly, desolate ride and the road climbs steadily upward. The moonlight turns the hills into silver rocks and I never travel it without an awareness of how many have climbed that road through the endless ages.

As we drove along through the little villages, we saw two soldiers waiting for a lift and invited them to ride with us. One of them, a Moroccan whose parents had come to Israel some ten years before, had reached the ripe old age of twenty-one and was now on a ten-hour leave from his unit, rushing home to see his wife, who was going to have a baby momentarily. "Are you afraid of the Arabs?" I asked him.

"Afraid of the Arabs?" he repeated, looking at me as though the bats in my belfry were clearly visible. He was disdainful. "Why should anyone be afraid of the Arabs?" He had been mobilized and had fought in the desert for many days; his chief worry was how he could face his wife with his unshaven face.

The other soldier was a Sabra. In Israel, to be a Sabra— a native-born Israeli—is very much like being able to say in the U.S. that your ancestors came over on the *Mayflower*. He was a good deal older than his companion, about twenty-eight or twenty-nine, and teased him laughingly: "*Schlemiel*, if you wore a beard like I do, you'd have no trouble; you wouldn't have to worry about how you looked."

We dropped the two soldiers off in the darkened streets of Jerusalem and found our way to the King David Hotel. I remembered it well from other days and other times, when, under the English, no one was allowed into the dining room without formal dress and all the other regalia of social propriety. By now I was exhausted and didn't give two pins for what anyone thought of my appearance. All I really wanted in the world was a cold drink and some sleep.

As soon as we had checked in I called Room Service and made my simple request. A most polite voice responded with deep regret: "I am sorry, Madame. We have no room service. All our waiters are in the Army."

## ✖ TWO

# Rachel's Tomb

WITH A FEW HOURS' SLEEP behind me, I set out to establish contact with the authorities next morning. I had all sorts of letters of introduction, but I quickly found in effect the same old conditions that always prevail when I am out to get a story: nothing was to be done for me except what I could manage to do for myself. The man I was supposed to get in touch with—who was going to take care of everything for me—was very polite, the soul of infinite courtesy. Before leaving Cleveland I had arranged with him to have my military pass ready and interviews set up.

"Oh yes, Miss Fuldheim. I remember very well. We have everything arranged. All you have to do is call Mr. So-and-So, and he will take care of everything you want."

I called Mr. So-and-So, who said, "Why, how very nice

to have you here, Miss Fuldheim! If you will just call Mr. So-and-So, he will take care of everything you want." I called Mr. So-and-So the third and found that he, too, was delighted by my presence on the scene, and that I was to call Mr. So-and-So the fourth, who would be happy to take care of everything. By that time I knew I was on the old familiar bureaucratic merry-go-round and that I would have to get off it if I was to accomplish my goal.

I had seen a fellow Clevelander, Max Ratner, in the lobby earlier. Mr. Ratner, who has a number of factories in Israel, is a slight man of tremendous energy and kindness. He was going into Jordan by auto that day to visit Hebron and Beersheba. He generously invited Al Rosen and me to join him, and we jumped at the opportunity.

It was hotter than Hades, and the car was not air-conditioned. Middle Eastern heat can be savage, and I was convinced at the moment that until the hot countries make air conditioning universal they are not going to progress. Heat and sand are a specially cruel combination. An Israeli armored car accompanied us through the Jordanian towns. (Al Rosen had promised the manager of the station, whom I had literally browbeaten into giving me this assignment, that I would not take any imprudent chances. He kept his word and would not proceed without an escort of some kind.)

The Arabs had been informed that if they would surrender their guns, knives, and ammunition, no questions would be asked; the weapons would simply be picked up by the Israelis. But none were to be hidden in homes. In a number of instances Jordanians had not turned over their arms; when this fact was discovered, the Israeli Army immediately had the occupants removed and the house blown up.

We drove through the streets of Bethlehem and noticed sullen-looking Arab bystanders, although we saw no sign of snipers, and came to the cave in which so many millennia ago Jacob had buried his beloved second wife, Rachel. (Apparently Rachel had fallen ill during a journey and Jacob had bought this cave for her burial place.) It is not likely that Jacob would have approved of the beggars, the Arabs, or the sightseers crowding into the cave this Sunday morning.

I must confess that I had no feeling of religious fervor as I entered the dirty cave. The only thing that could be said for it was that it was cool; it was a relief to get away from the heat and dust of the desert. But with the carnival atmosphere outside I wouldn't have been surprised to find hawkers inside selling lemonade and what-not. I hope that someday the cave will be cleaned up and made a dignified historic shrine. Even so, it is something of an awesome experience to stand in a cave in the walls of which are buried the ashes of someone who has been dead for many centuries and whose memory has been kept alive longer than that of the Pharaohs.

"Rachel old girl," I thought to myself, "if you were alive I wonder what we could talk about." I wondered if she knew the seething sense of victory storming through the heat, in the hearts not only of the Israelis but of all Jews, because of the valor and the courage and the extraordinary skill of the modern Israelis. Never before in all of history (and certainly it is not likely ever to happen again) has a small nation with only two and one-half million people hewn a victory out of incredible odds within six days as did the Israelis against a hundred million Arabs dedicated—according to their own statement—not only to the destruction of the State of Israel but also to the annihilation of all its citizens. Nasser had said that the Mediterranean would be their burying ground. The Israeli answer was that the Mediterranean would turn red with Arab blood before this could happen.

In the intolerable heat we drove on to Ramalah, Nablas, and Jenin. It is hardly surprising that we experienced some apprehension, for we were met everywhere by curious and hostile looks on the part of the Arabs standing in their doorways as we passed with our armed guides. I wondered what the Arabs were thinking as they gazed at us. Al Rosen insisted that it was my white dress and red hair that attracted their attention. If so, they were not viewing us with any enthusiasm, and I had the feeling that they would not have minded decorating my dress with mud.

These Jordanian towns are dusty and dirty, with no plants or shrubs or trees anywhere. We did spot a few magnificent villas, which obviously belonged to wealthy Arabs. There must have been some very rich Arabs in Ramalah; I noticed a sign reading MERCEDES-BENZ DEALER. Indeed, one of the sheikhs complained bitterly because twenty Mercedes-Benz buses he had bought were parked in Jerusalem and now that the Israelis had taken Jerusalem he was sure he would never get them back. He estimated his loss to be in excess of a million dollars.

Even the magnificent villas had no shrubs or trees surrounding them, and there are no sidewalks. Community pride seems lacking among the Arabs I saw. They are dirty partly because there is a limited amount of water. They are poor because the wealth of the country is controlled by a relatively few men—it is reported that fifty sheikhs own most of the arable land in Jordan. The preponderance of the population are peasants who barely eke out a livelihood. The middle class as we know it in the United States is nonexistent, and until there is a middle class with a purchasing power the Arabs will never raise their standard of living.

The women walk barefoot with dusty black veils over their faces. I personally can't understand why they have to hide their faces; they don't look very alluring to me, but of course I am not an Arab male. Bundles are perched upon their heads as they walk the dusty roads while the men ride donkeys. We are told that this practice of carrying a bundle on the head produces a fine carriage, but for me the price would be too great to pay for an upright posture. I'll just keep my American slouch and continue to wonder how the Arabs can ever produce a modern civilization while their women are treated as though they were slaves. No country in this century has succeeded in civilizing its people as long as its women are treated as second- and third-class citizens, fit only for the bedroom and hard work.

One old Arab woman followed me with such tenacity she made a pest of herself. She was carrying a burlap bag and was begging for money or for food. She wore no veil, but she had neither beauty nor sex appeal to hide; she was toothless, dirty, and a sad-looking creature.

The drive was hot and dusty, discouraging and enlightening at the same time, for it spelled out for me more clearly than ever before the difference between the progressiveness of the Israelis and the static condition of the economy and educational system of their Arab neighbors. The problem of communicating is immensely complicated by the fact that the two peoples are living in different eras: the Israelis in the twentieth century, the Arabs in the Middle Ages.

# THREE

# The Price of War

MILITARY EXPERTS say a country is defeated in war if it loses six or seven per cent of its population. German losses during World War II never reached as much as ten per cent, but in June 1967 the Israelis told me—calmly and apparently without any feeling that it was an unusual statement—that if necessary they would have continued fighting even with fifty per cent of their people lost. For them this was not an ordinary kind of war; this was a war for survival. The German defeat by the Allies in 1945 did not mean death for all Germans, any more than the Japanese defeat meant death for all Japanese. But an Israeli defeat in June 1967 would have meant death for most of the nation's people; Nasser had proclaimed over and over—as other Arab leaders had—that the Arab goal was the annihilation of Israel. So it is not hard to understand why the Israelis were prepared, if necessary, to have taken a forty- or fifty-per-cent loss.

Israel was sharply aware of what it considered John Foster Dulles' mistake in the War of 1956 and was determined not to have its victory invalidated as it had been then. When Dulles and then-President Dwight Eisenhower forced the British and French to leave Egypt in 1956 (and in the process destroyed British Prime Minister Anthony Eden politically), Nasser became the victor although he had been defeated militarily, and a vacuum was created in the Middle East. Into this vacuum the Soviet Union moved quickly and for ten years poured incredible amounts of ammunition and money into Egypt and the other Arab countries.

Whatever the Russians said publicly, they must certainly have been enraged privately at the field ineptness of the Arab world they had equipped and so confidently defended in the United Nations. That defense had not been one of dignity, but downright lies, without finesse and with vulgarity against Israel, even stooping—as Soviet UN Ambassador Federenko did at one point—to compare Israel's conduct with that of the Nazis. The world was treated to the spectacle of a powerful nation squirming in an attempt to salvage some prestige out of the enormity of the defeat of the Arab world.

The Hadassah Hospital in Tel Aviv is magnificent, a monument to the generosity of the American Jewish women who raised the funds to build and equip and maintain it. The finest doctors in the world staff it; if I had to be ill anywhere but in the United States, I would hope it would be at this hospital. It stands on a high hill amid flowering shrubs and trees. The corridors were filled with friends and families waiting to see the wounded soldiers.

I visited the hospital because even the decisions to move quickly and prevent the size and power of the Russian-backed armies from overwhelming the nation did not spare the Israelis from paying a bitter price for victory. Six hundred seventy-nine Israelis were killed in the war, which may not sound like much. After all, in the United States before a holiday such as July Fourth, the National Safety Council predicts that almost a thousand Americans will be killed. Somehow being slaughtered by that lethal weapon, the automobile, doesn't seem to shock Americans. But in terms of the population of the United States, the Israeli loss is the same as if sixty-two thousand Americans had been killed and more than three hundred thousand wounded in a six-day war.

In one of the wards a young soldier—he was about twenty-one—who had an abdominal wound was very excited: he was going to be married in about half an hour. He explained to me that he was not going to let a war or any Arab prevent him from keeping his wedding date. He was a handsome youngster; I was tempted to lean over and kiss him. His parents and family were all assembled and then the bride came in, in her veil and bridal dress. The wedding ceremony was performed, and she spent her honeymoon sitting next to her groom's bed holding his hand. No wonder the parents of the young couple had trouble hiding their tears! Young love should know happiness and the sweetness that comes with the first days of a marriage, but these two will be experiencing their first months in this hospital ward, and no one really knows whether the young soldier will remain a cripple.

Many a time since I have wondered if he will recover and if someday, in an Israel free of threats, the young soldier and his bride will tell their children about how their marriage took place in the Hadassah Hospital in Tel Aviv on a hot June morning in 1967.

In the corridor an American man was walking up and down, weeping. He turned to me without an introduction, apparently realizing I was an American, and moaned, "You know where my boy is, my beautiful boy, my beautiful boy? He's up there—," pointing to the operating room. "They are taking off his leg. My beautiful boy," he said, "will have only one leg." An Israeli friend was trying to console him (he had his arm around him): "It's all right, it's all right! So he has only one leg, so what? What's so wonderful about a two-legged man? His wife will love him even though he has only one leg."

Walking up and down the corridor, in his grief the man would turn to anyone to tell his story. He had come from Brooklyn to visit his son, a doctor. The doctor of course was mobilized and was wounded while in one of the helicopters attending some injured soldiers who were being carried back to their base.

In one of the other wards some of the young men were playing the guitar while others were amusing themselves with a set of dominoes so old I expected the board to fall apart. I tried to get a story from them, but they were very matter-of-fact about the war. When I asked the standard question, "Were you afraid?," they shrugged their shoulders. One of them, a pilot, answered "Yes, I guess so, but I was more nervous waiting to get into my plane. Once I was at the controls my nervousness disappeared. I noticed that the skies were orange and golden and I felt sorry that some of the Egyptian fliers would have to die that morning."

"Why were you so sure they would die? Weren't you afraid that you would be killed?" I asked.

He looked up with a cheerful grin and said, "Well, you

see I was right; I am still alive. It was the Egyptian fliers who were killed." I sat down to play a game of checkers with him. He beat me; the other men in the ward tried to console me by saying "You have to be a flier to play checkers."

I invited them all to visit me in Cleveland. They assured me they would, particularly if the invitation included round-trip tickets. They wanted to know about the girls they would meet. "I want a blonde one," the flier said. "I yearn for blue eyes and golden hair."

The guitar player said, "I'll come with my guitar and I will sing to the girls."

"You better come with money," spoke up one of the young men, whose arm was bandaged. "I understand American girls are only interested in chaps who are rich."

The guitar player was undaunted. "I don't have to be rich, I'm a hero."

A sardonic laugh followed. "Some hero! In the midst of the battle he gets an ulcer attack."

I waved good-bye and left with my own parting shot: "I've got an ulcer too, but I can't play the guitar."

Three patients in one corner of the ward made me think of the Three Musketeers—one for all and all for one—a captain, a corporal, and a medic.

The Captain and the Corporal had been walking along the Suez Canal as part of an advance platoon. "Hey, Cap," called the Corporal, "am I wounded? I feel some blood." The Captain looked, changed his gun to his other hand, and put his hand over and into the wound to keep it from bleeding too profusely. "You better stop here," he said. "No," answered the Corporal, "I'm going on with you." So they walked with the Captain's hand in the Corporal's wound until the Corporal fell from loss of blood. Eventually a medic came by and the Corporal was lifted into a helicopter and flown back for first aid.

Then the medic returned to find the Captain wounded and took him back, also for first aid. Once more the medic returned to see if further aid were needed; this time it was he who was wounded and, in turn, flown back to base.

So the three found themselves in the same ward. "Gentlemen," I said, "I salute you as conquerors of Egypt." The Corporal answered he felt that he had been cheated; what he wanted to do, so he could boast about it, was to swim in the Suez Canal, so long closed to the Israelis.

The Captain said, "In your condition you would have turned the Canal red with your blood. Do you know," he said, turning to me, "that in Jordan the Arabs had bags ready to be filled with loot which they expected they would plunder from the vanquished Jews? They had been told that the Jews would be defeated and forced to yield their possessions."

"Don't get yourself excited," said the Medic. "They didn't win and they didn't fill the bags because our military strategy was based on surprise—the unexpected and swiftness.

"I suppose you are familiar," he continued, "with General Dayan's military philosophy, which is daring and unorthodox. If those dumb Arabs had ever read Dayan's own report of the war of 1956, they would have known that our strategy in this war would also be to do the unexpected. It's what we did in 1956; that's why we won then and now."

At that moment a nurse came in; the war was forgotten, sex reared its beautiful head, and the three of them gave their undivided attention to a lovely pair of legs and a blonde head. "Tell me, pretty maid," said the Corporal, "where do you come from?"

"Don't pay any attention to him," said the Captain. "He's delirious."

"Certainly," retorted the Corporal, "I'm delirious at the sight of your beauty, Nurse. The Captain is just jealous of my virile good looks."

Then the Medic piped in his two cents' worth: "You're wasting your time, fellows. I'm the only unmarried one, so the arena is mine."

The nurse stuck a thermometer into his mouth and said, "Now the arena is mine, and anyhow I am married—and my husband is as jealous as an Arab. He even wants me to wear a veil."

I went out laughing.

How wonderful they were in maintaining their high spirits!

# ✪ FOUR

# A Tattoo Number

I SAT DOWN on a bench in a corridor in Tel Aviv's Hadassah Hospital next to a woman who moved over to make room for me, a gaunt figure with coal-black hair streaked with gray and a sad face with eyes that never smiled. She must have been about sixty-five. I started to talk with her—the Israelis are an outgoing people and enter into conversation very easily—and asked her why she was there.

"My grandson was wounded and I am waiting to go into the room," she answered. "The nurse is dressing his wounds." Every other sentence was "Thank God, he wasn't killed"; "Thank God, the boy came back to us"; she must have used at least a dozen *Thank Gods*, and it seemed to me by that time she had really shown her gratitude to God sufficiently.

When she moved her hand over her knee, I noticed the marks imprinted in the skin, insignia of the concentration camp. The tattoo marks are recognizable. I thought what a great story she must have and hoped that in some way I could get her to talk. As she felt my eyes searching the tattoo marks, she said with sort of a wry smile, "Yes, I was in a concentration camp when I was my grandson's age. I spent three years there. I was strong and I was healthy and I did the work, and I was used by the Nazi soldiers. Every time they touched me I gave an inner prayer to God: 'Please let them fall down dead now!' But they didn't fall down dead, but I didn't die either."

After she had been freed from the concentration camp what she wanted more than anything else was to get away from humanity. She hated all mankind, but fortunately for her she came to Israel and found some peace of mind. She married an Israeli, and as the years passed some of the brutality and horror of the days of the concentration camp were erased from her mind. She told me that when the war broke out and her daughter was crying because her son had to go, she took her grandson in her arms and said, "Hyman, I don't know if the Lord will bring you back or not, but at least the Lord is giving you a chance to fight for your life. When I was your age, I couldn't fight for my life. They didn't even give me a chance to do that. They let me live in shame and in horror.

"And you know what that young grandson said to me? 'Never mind, Grandma, this will never happen again. There will be no concentration camps. We defeated them twice before, Grandma, and we are going to do it again. No one, Nasser or anyone, is going to shove us around.'

"My grandson," she added, "is very handsome; he looks like my father, who died in Auschwitz." I knew then why her eyes were sad.

I must say that the Israeli soldiers are a cocky lot. They are strong; they look vital, and many of them are quite handsome. What is even more extraordinary is that the Army is made up of men from a hundred different countries. I talked to Israeli soldiers who had come from Uruguay, South Africa, Finland, Sweden, Morocco, Germany, Iraq—name at least a hundred different countries and you will find someone from that land who has come to live in Israel. The astounding fact is that with all these differences they were able to unify in time of war. It is also true that the first generation that migrated to Israel was divided by language and culture from the newcomers.

The Eastern Jew had little in common with the Western Jew, and the transition was difficult for both. For example, the Yemeni people had never seen an airplane; they really thought it was a big bird. The women knew nothing about diapers. They could not sew. They suffered needless hardships because they did not know any better. They were not familiar with much of the Western world's technical know-how.

It is different with the children. They have gone to school, and a homogeneous culture is developing that is peculiarly Israeli. The schools and the Army serve as leavening agents. For example, all children are taught English from grade six on—it is mandatory. In addition they are exposed to the use of English in the Army.

There are no ghetto Jews in Israel, none of these small, narrow-chested Jews who dwelt in the shadows of countless ghettos for so many hundreds of years. These young men are stalwart, strong, big-muscled. These are men who have worked the hard earth with their bare hands and who can do such things as fix a car or a tractor. They are technically efficient as well as educated. Even before the establishment of the State of Israel there was a university in Palestine. Today Israel boasts six or seven institutions of higher learning. Their famous Technion, frequently compared to the Massachusetts Institute of Technology, has flowered into one of the great intellectual and scientific centers of the world—in a nation that is twenty years old and has a population of only two and a half million.

And, above all else, there is among these men a spirit of bravery that is touching. They are afraid of nothing. I'd ask them "Aren't you afraid?" and they would laugh at me. "Afraid? Of whom, the Arabs?" And they would laugh again.

I remember being stopped at a roadblock on our way to Ramalah and talking with the four soldiers on duty there. They were like American boys, with the same sense of humor. They insisted that we contribute to the collection they were getting up to bring Nasser's children to Israel so they could receive a good education. They also wanted to know if we could give them the name of a clever attorney. They wanted to know how to set up a corporation, since they were planning to buy the Pyramids from the Israeli government, which was certainly going to obtain them in lieu of reparations. They told me with a grin that they were preparing to sell stock in the Pyramids and pay dividends from the proceeds of the concession stands they would establish in the sands nearby. Hot dogs, lemonade, and souvenirs of the war. I immediately put in my bid to buy a hundred shares at any price.

The similarity between these boys and Americans is very great. When we became a nation we, too, were made up of people who had come from many lands. The immigrants to America were the malcontents, the rebels, the dreamers. Few nobles or wealthy people emigrated. Only those who were dissatisfied with their status in the country of their birth, only those who wanted a better life for themselves and their children, who yearned to be free of the tyranny of kings, for the right to think and worship as they believed journeyed in the boats that took months to cross the ocean. They were the adventurous and the adventurers; fearless, willing to take chances, ready to labor and hungry to achieve, gutty and high-spirited. They made an amorphous group, but they melted into one and became one nation; they made a virgin continent theirs; they filled it with wealth as a result of their labors, and they made it free because they were rebels and nonconformists. This is one of the reasons the United States has produced such tremendous wealth: the adventurers who came here were not afraid of taking chances. The Carnegies, the Rockefellers, the McCormicks, the Astors, the Seligmans were men of daring.

A similar situation exists in Israel; her people also came from a variety of lands, and only the strong and adventurous came to Israel. With their bare hands, with their brawn, and with their sweat they have built a blooming land out of a desert! They knew that they must conquer the desert or the desert would negate all their hopes to be a nation.

There is one significant difference between the United States and Israel. The Israelis have one thing in common: their Bible, which is their history book; along with this comes a literary tradition inherent in their Bible. The children study the Bible as we do our history books.

And the Israelis have another thing in common—a background of persecution, for not one of the Jews, even those born in Israel, is completely free of the memory of barbarous and stupid persecution. The survivors of the century-old persecutions were the physically strong, the smart, and the adventurous ones. Which is not to deny that among them are some who were just plain lucky, but most were the strong in mind and body; these were the survivors, the progenitors of modern Israel.

The branded Israeli woman invited me to go into the ward with her to see her grandson. "Look, Hyman," she said, "I've brought you a visitor." Her sad eyes were shining with love and admiration for her grandson. "You know," she added, "he is six feet tall."

"Oh come on, Grandma," he teased her. "You know I'm all body and no brain." The woman leaned over and kissed the top of his head. "Hyman, she's an American," she said, turning to me.

"So," he said, "someday we will go to America, Grandma, you and I. But you'll have to fly, you know."

"Listen to him," she said. "He says he will take his old grandma with him, but he thinks I'm afraid to fly. But with you Hyman, I will go anywhere, even in a plane."

With a mock groan he turned on his side. One arm and one leg had apparently suffered gunfire wounds. "What a *bubba* I have; she has to go with me everywhere I go. I'm surprised you didn't come in with a gun and fight with my division." There was clearly great affection between the two of them. But before she could answer him a young woman of twenty-two or twenty-three with limpid black eyes and coal-black hair came in carrying some flowers in her arms. The young soldier's face lit up with joy, and he extended his uninjured arm and pulled her to him. I stepped out softly; he never noticed my leaving. His grandmother followed me.

"I'll sit out here for a while on the bench," she said. "They don't need me."

# ✖ FIVE

# The Israeli Army

GAMAL ABDEL NASSER had boasted that he would wipe out Israel within twelve days. Underneath these boasts was the fact that Israel remained a symbol of humiliation to the Arabs. The land had been regarded as virtually worthless when the Arabs sold it to the early Zionist settlers. Sheer guts, backbreaking work, and a dream had turned what the Arabs had so disdainfully looked upon as rock and sand into the most valuable piece of real estate in the Middle East.

Through the years they labored, these Jews who paid cold cash for the land they bought from the Arabs. They stole nothing, they were not raiders. They bought the land the Arabs sold willingly enough, and over the years they heard constantly the threat that they were to be exterminated. Nasser's commitment to the destruction of Israel became a litany repeated until apparently Nasser began to be intoxicated by his own song. Twice the Israeli farmers put down their plows and their seed and went out to defend themselves—in 1948 and in 1956. Twice they proved that they could and would stand guard over the sacred land they had nurtured with their sweat, their brawn, and their brains.

When the Arabs and Russians stood ready to catapult the world into another war in May 1967, and Israel was surrounded on all sides by the might of Russian ammunition and Arab armies, the Israelis answered in Ben-Gurion's words: "If we wait a moment longer we will be like the Jews who walked obediently to their deaths in the Nazi extermination camps, and if Israel goes the same way there is no future hope for humanity." David Ben-Gurion, that doughty old warrior who, like some gnarled oak tree, has shed his wisdom and his stolid courage over the people of the Holy Land, had given voice to the Israelis' resolute determination.

In a manner of speaking, if the Western world can get any comfort out of this, the Israeli victory vindicated the hope that man is evolving—for it was spirit, morale, *élan*, and brains that won this spectacular and unparalleled brief war. This was an army that was a hundred per cent literate. Egypt and Syria have thirty per cent literacy, Iraq and Saudi Arabia even less. (How can an illiterate army in modern times fight a literate one? If a nation is literate, training is fast and thorough, and skilled mechanics know how to operate complex equipment.)

The Israeli Army itself is in great measure responsible for the nation's high literacy rate. The State of Israel did not have an easy time of it; many of the Jews who came from the African and Asian ghettos were illiterate. The

Army became the biggest educational institution in the country, for it taught the Moroccan, Iraqi, and the Yemenite Jews how to read and write. This is no longer a problem, of course, because all Israeli children are now required to go to school.

In 1967 the Army was made up chiefly of reservists. There were five times as many reservists as regulars; they looked shabby; there was no shine and trim to them. They were not properly dressed and they arrived in all kinds of civilian vehicles—market trucks, delivery wagons, fruit trucks, taxicabs. Buses took reservists to their units, although many simply hitchhiked to their posts. Spit and polish were absent. This was a citizens' army that could not afford to waste ammunition, gasoline, or supplies.

When the Israeli forces took off on that fateful June morning to destroy and break the Egyptian air force, they left behind them exactly twelve planes to defend the whole State of Israel! They lacked the opulent and lavish equipment of the Arabs; Russia had not been their godfather, constantly sending gifts to them.

They knew each other; many of the men called the officers by their first names. It was *Moshe,* not *Dayan.* Men and officers ate together during the war. There were no batmen to polish officers' boots. The soldier's job was to save Israel, not to wait on officers. This was no army dedicated to military glory. They knew they would win; the question was how quickly could they finish the war and get back to their regular jobs.

Some amusing incidents were bound to happen in this egalitarian army. General Abraham Yoffe said that once, early in the battle, he heard somebody ask permission to take a route other than the one his platoon had been directed to take. Asked why, the footsoldier said, "Well, there is a bunch of Arab tanks over there and I think we ought to take it."

"I told him," said the General, "to stick his nose into his own business and not interfere with his company commander. They kept trying to find their own individual enemy and to destroy him. When we hit the Suez Canal one of my commanders sent word asking permission to wash his feet. That's how I knew we had arrived in the Suez. My answer was *no,* and I don't know yet whether his feet are washed."

In Israel almost everyone serves in the Army. When the war broke out the women of Israel were so desperate in their desire to do something to help that they began baking cakes and baked so many that the officials finally cried "Please, an army cannot fight on cakes. Don't bake any more!"

The Post Office was without men; all the mailmen were in the war, so the Boy Scouts volunteered to sort and deliver the mail. It was really something to see a Boy Scout carrying mailbags and delivering the mail, performing the jobs older men had been doing before the war. No one, unless he has lived in a country where everyone is involved in war, understands what the draft meant. It included everybody.

The army consists of sixty thousand regulars and about two hundred four thousand reservists. War mobilization puts ten per cent of the population in uniform, a feat matched by few other nations, if any. Regulars and reservists are ready to fight at once if war breaks out; they do not have to have a thirty- or sixty-day mobilization period.

All reservists take thirty days' field training a year plus one day a month for weapons duty and target practice; sergeants and officers have an additional day of training a month. The reservists as well as the regular personnel know all about the newest weapons. The regulars keep the weapons clean and periodically warm up the jeep engines. They check the tank engines' radio equipment. Even first-aid packaged drugs are checked to make sure they have not aged beyond their usefulness. A reservist who in civilian life drives a tractor can expect on mobilization to drive his tractor, with a trailer, to his unit; they will probably put a tank on the trailer when they move to the front lines, in this way saving the fuel the tank would use up. I saw ice-cream trucks and diaper trucks, plastered with mud as camouflage, carrying rations to troops in the desert. Reservists are mobilized by radio or code phrases flashed on movie screens. Imagine turning on your radio and hearing "Good morning to Open Window, Wedding March, Sweet Honey, Machine Oil, Zionist Fervor . . ." code phrases indicating what groups have been called up.

The efficiency of the Regular Army and of the reserves has been demonstrated again and again. There is no pageantry in this Army, no fife and drum, no dress parades. While officers are treated with respect, there are few salutes. Many officers use their own cars for transportation, smearing mud over the surface for camouflage.

In peacetime, of course, the officers eat separately. This army is unique in the fact that the command "forward" is never heard as it is in other armies, never! Because no officer ever orders an Israeli private to advance where the officer does not. The officer always goes first; the words heard are "Follow me." As a result officers made up one-third of the fatalities and wounded. This is what makes the Israeli Army different from any other army. The officers do not save themselves, they go right in where the fighting is grimmest. The uniforms are shabby, but the spirit is rare and unconquerable.

Quite different are the Arab officers, who arrived with white silk scarves and even white gloves. It is difficult to believe this, but one Egyptian officer, a brigadier general handed his Israeli captors a calling card containing the information that he was "the Military Naval and Air Attaché, U.A.R. Embassy, Pakistan." Brigadier General Ariel Sharon, the Israeli officer who was handed the elegantly engraved card, was astonished. "They may have calling cards," he said, "but they cannot fight."

Apparently the Arab General had only one personal regret; he told his captors "I lost my luggage, which I bought in London a month ago, and also my transistor radio." He quite freely explained what had happened. He said he had been commanding an armored brigade. He was ordered to retreat after an Israeli air attack, so he abandoned his tanks without further ado and fell back with his brigade intact. His troops panicked and fled when they stumbled on some Israeli roadblocks. The General, his callings cards kept carefully in his pocket, hid from the Israelis for several days, but thirst and hunger made him surrender, and he acknowledged that the Israeli patrol which had captured him had treated him with kindness.

## ✸ SIX

# The Tenth Battalion Comes Home

I STOOD on the street and watched the Tenth Battalion come back. Tank after tank, truck after truck loaded with Israeli soldiers flying the white flag with the blue Star of David high above their heads, the flags of the vanquished in their hands. The trucks were mainly captured Russian trucks. Here were men, almost blackened by the desert sun, in shabby uniform riding on Russian tanks and trucks they had picked up in the desert from the fleeing Arabs. I stood there, and I wept for a reason I can't quite explain. Perhaps it was because these men had saved a tiny nation from annihilation. They were the civilians who had left their shops and their families, even as American men in the Revolutionary War had followed George Washington. Perhaps the thing that moved me most was that most of these men were sucking away at a Popsicle that had been distributed to them by someone. They were thirsty, and I suppose the ice confection felt good against their dry lips. I must admit I found myself dumfounded watching a triumphant army returning with lemon-flavored Popsicles in their mouths.

I was torn with sobs as I watched the Tenth Battalion come riding back in the captured tanks and trucks. Why? Why were tears running down the cheeks of Al Rosen? We wept because it was not just the Tenth Battalion of the Israeli Army that was returning; marching with them were the dead, the million, million dead. I wept for the anguish of those millions; I sobbed for the million children who were placed into gas chambers. I wept for those burned in the ovens at Auschwitz. I wept for the dwellers and the tortured in the Polish ghettos. I wept for the branded arms of eight million Jews. I wept for their anguish and for their broken pride and their sullied womanhood. I wept for mankind's infinite capacity for wickedness, and I wept with passion at the sight of these bronzed men burnt by the desert sun, these men dusty with the sands of the desert, these men holding guns in their hands.

These men are a new breed of Jews, who have stood up to fate and announced, "We gave the world thinkers, scientists, creators, musicians, but the world's answer was death, death to the Jews. We turned our swords into ploughshares, but the world was not content. Now we, the new Jews, forged out of adversity—for only the ingenious and the resourceful survived the bitter persecutions— have set aside our ploughshares. We have taken the avenging sword in our hands. Life shall not be denied us until the last of us have fallen. We shall not die ignominiously again. No more gas chambers, for if we die we take our enemies with us through the door of death." This is the new Jew. This is the conquering Jew, the victor.

And so I wept for those whose ghosts and whose memory marched with the Tenth Battalion on that boulevard in Tel Aviv on that June day.

# SEVEN

# Al Rosen Is Always Thirsty

AL ROSEN suffered a sustained and unbroken thirst; no matter how many beers, how many glasses of tea, how many cold drinks he consumed, he was constantly thirsty. To keep up with him I drank so much tea that I began to feel like a teapot, and I was sure I was turning the color of tea.

"It's the desert air," he would explain solemnly. One morning we stopped at a motel not too far from Tel Aviv, to have a beer. The motel was run by a man who was English by birth, though he had lived in Israel for thirty years. He had a cheerful face and the protruding stomach of the well-fed. The dining room was immaculate. The linen cloths were white; the silver was shining; there

**47**

were flowers on the table. The mirror behind the bar was covered with ornamented recipes for exotic drinks. There was no sign of the war here, for outside the garden was in full bloom, but there were no guests occupying any of the rooms. During the war people were not taking vacations. The proprietor was whistling and polishing the glasses on the bar when we entered and Al ordered his inevitable beer. I challenged the proprietor with "What are you so happy about?"

"Why shouldn't I be happy?" he said, as he continued shining the glasses on the bar so that they sparkled even more brightly. "I just made a million dollars today."

I must have looked startled. I didn't expect a motel-keeper in the suburbs of Tel Aviv to have made a million dollars, at least not during the war. Perplexed, I asked, "Do you mind telling me how you made a million dollars?"

"No, I don't mind," he answered. "You see, yesterday the Arabs were coming. They were going to take my property. Today the Israeli Army is victorious; the Arabs are not in Tel Aviv and my property is mine, so I am worth at least a million dollars compared to yesterday." So we drank to his good fortune, a double beer to celebrate.

"But," he added, "don't think I am satisfied. I am writing a letter to the Government. I don't approve of the Government at all and I am writing them a letter. I am saying to them: 'What is the matter with you? You don't think I am any good any more? I was good enough to be a captain and to fight in the last war, but now I am fifty-eight years old so I'm on the ash heap. So you don't need me, do you? Why couldn't you have asked me to run a truck for you, to do something? What right have you to act as though I weren't a citizen of this country, an Israeli? I want to call your attention to the fact that I am still a good healthy Israeli and I don't like it at all that you eliminated me from this war.'" And he wasn't fooling. He was indignant

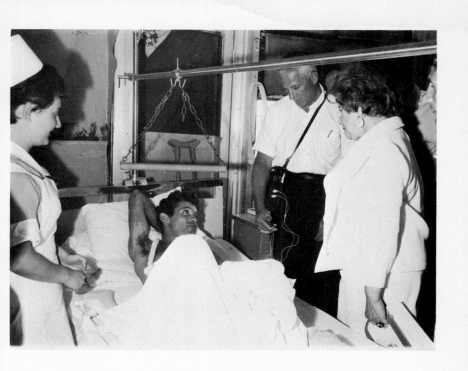

*The price of war—Hadassah Hospital, Tel Aviv.*

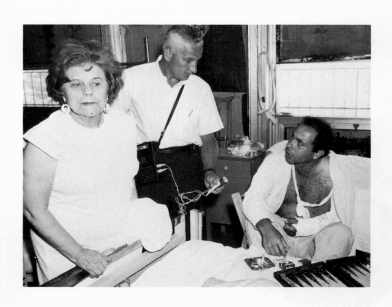

*The victorious 10th Battalion, with captured tanks, returns to Tel Aviv.*

*John Wayne, Israeli style.*

*Twentieth century meets 14th century.*

*Israel built the port Ashdod, a city of almost 20,000, in less than seven years.*

*Jews, not Arabs, on a street in Ashdod.*

*Mandelbaum Gate, Jerusalem.*

*Israeli soldiers in Jerusalem. The man on my right has the handle of a mine detector in his hand.*

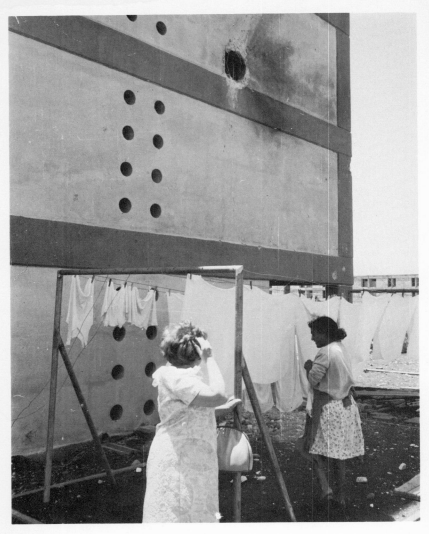

*Air conditioning, Arab style, in Jerusalem.*

*General Moshe Dayan refuses an interview,*
*King David Hotel, Jerusalem.*

*Mayor "Teddy" Kollek, now mayor of all Jerusalem, talks with Al Rosen and me on the top of Jerusalem's Municipal Building.*

*Yossie Levi, on the right, guards the ramparts.*

that he hadn't been used, and he was almost in tears when he explained how he had been snubbed, how his services had not been utilized.

His happy-faced wife, portly as her husband, was standing by, smiling. I turned to her and said, "Do you agree with him?"

"My husband," she said, "may he live long, is always right." I laughed and said, "You really mean that?"

"Well," she answered with a shrug, "most of the time I do. But you see we have lived here over thirty years; our children were born here. My husband was in the 1956 war and we both wanted to do something. My husband is strong; he could have done something. He is smart and he is a good fighter, and we feel responsible for Israel, too. But I said to him 'Stop eating yourself up, if they don't want you, they don't want you, so what can you do about it?'"

"What kind of a philosophy is that?" her husband thundered. "Women," he said to Al Rosen, "who can understand them?"

Al Rosen, trying to look sympathetic, started to answer, but before he could the proprietor's wife turned away, shrugging her shoulders. "I understand you," she said. "Why aren't you smart enough to understand me."

It was not difficult to understand either of them. To understand the spirit of this couple was to understand the spirit of the Israeli people during those critical days before the war when they knew they could rely only on themselves for courage and the strength to survive.

I took Al's arm and we walked through the door into the hot, desert morning.

# EIGHT

# The One-Eyed General

DURING THE BITTER HOURS when the Israeli people were waiting for the Government to take some action and when there was genuine fear among the people that the Government was too dilatory, a wave of excitement swept through the country with the announcement that Dayan had been made Minister of Defense. General Moshe Dayan had already become a legend. He had led the Israelis to victory in 1956, and the announcement that he had been made Minister of Defense was tantamount to saying to the world, "We will now take the first step against those who are threatening to destroy us." (It was reported that the Egyptians were unhappy at the fact that Dayan was in control.)

The Egyptians had seven divisions in Sinai. The Israelis had only three divisions. (Once when Napoleon was discussing a projected battle with his marshals, one of the marshals pointed out that Napoleon had only ten divisions and the enemy twenty. Whereupon Napoleon drew himself up to his full five three or four and with a withering look addressed the marshal: "We have ten divisions and myself. That means we have twenty divisions.") Dayan was at that moment worth at least a half a dozen divisions. What chemistry draws everyone to a man? What is it that makes a man magnetic? Why are certain men marked to become heroes of the people? General Itzack Rabin is said to have been the brains behind the military strategy, and he is a great military general. Yet Dayan is the hero with a quality of magnetism that is as rare as it is exciting.

Dayan is not handsome, but his mark of distinction, the black patch over an eye that is missing, identifies him and marks him as a romantic figure. He was born in 1915 on a kibbutz in the hot and humid Jordan valley along the Sea of Galilee. By the time he was twelve he was standing sentry duty against marauding Bedouins. It was here that he learned to speak Arabic fluently.

Under the British Captain Orde Wingate, he became a commando and at the age of twenty-two was made Wingate's second in command. Later he put the technique he learned from Wingate to the service of the Haganah group, which was outlawed by the British. He was captured by the British in 1939 and sentenced to five years in prison. Two years later he was released, and led fifty cloak-and-dagger commandos disguised as Arabs into Syria, where they gathered information for the British.

Dayan learned to know the Arabs—the way they think and the manner in which they react. In a World War II battle in Lebanon, Dayan was holding a telescope up to his left eye when a bullet caught the glass with a glancing blow, driving it into his eye socket. Ever since he has worn his distinguishing eye patch. In 1952 he attended the Senior Staff Officers' School in England and the following year he became Chief of Staff of the Israeli Army. As top commander Dayan insisted that every Israeli officer be trained either as a commando or a paratrooper. He himself chose the role of paratrooper and broke a leg in a jump in 1955.

In the 1956 war, Dayan's concept of military strategy brought about Israel's spectacular triumph; it was in this war that he displayed both the speed and surprise night movements he used again for his stunning triumph in June 1967. He is an individualist and fiercely independent. He does not drink and he does not smoke, but he does drink tea. I have seen him drink glass after glass of it.

Perhaps the most compelling compliment paid him was by American Lieutenant General Lewis Walt, who said, "He is a brilliant tactician and strategist. I would hate to have him on the other side."

The people of Israel were maddened at what they considered the Government's effort to talk, to conciliate, to persuade the Egyptians to go away. They felt that they were on the brink of disaster as they continued to wait for the United Nations to do something, as Premier Eshkol had been advised by the Western governments.

"Eshkol did not want me," General Dayan told an American reporter, "but the people wanted me. Eshkol wanted to make me Military Advisor, but I told him 'Either make me Minister of Defense or just give me the forces in the Negev and I will take care of the Egyptians.' " When Eshkol made this proposal the other members of his Government said, "To hell with it; we want Dayan."

Dayan announced that Israel was not only willing to

take the Arabs on alone, but that Israel did not want the soldiers of any other country getting killed to secure Israeli safety. The "hawks" had won. If Nasser had chosen the hour, the Israelis decided on the minute.

I tried to get an interview with Dayan. Even Mayor Kollek of Jerusalem used his efforts, but with no avail. At the moment Dayan was too busy. I sent him six enormous roses, one for each day of the war, but I have no way of knowing whether he ever received them. If he did he never told me about it. But one afternoon just before twilight, I walked onto the terrace of the King David Hotel, overlooking the garden. Here in 1948 I had been obliged to lie down on the ground because the snipers were shooting across the terrace. (This was when the Jews had been fighting to get the English to allow them to stay there.) On this same terrace I spoke to General Dayan. Not with much satisfaction, I must say, because he ordered tea and I assume he begrudged the time he gave me. I could hardly blame him. He was not only under tremendous pressure, but there was also the question of how far the civilian government would allow the military to go in expressing itself, and Dayan must have been in a difficult spot. He was the hero of the hour, but the Government did not propose to allow the military to make policy. If Dayan had come to the United States, I'm certain he would have been given a ticker-tape parade in New York, because he had captivated the imagination of the people. He had also given the Israeli Army an almost mystical belief in his ability.

While the world shivered with apprehension in the last days of May, at the catastrophe that awaited Israel, in one of the Israeli Government buildings, eighteen men were planning the campaign to the last detail. They knew exactly where they were going, how they were going, when they were going, and how long it would take them to win

the war. There was and still is the question of whether
the Israeli Government has the atom bomb. It was reported some months before the war broke out that certain
United States Government officials had been to Israel and
had received assurance from Israel that she would not
manufacture the atom bomb and that in return for that
assurance the United States offered Israel a guarantee of
her territorial integrity.

Whether this is just gossip or truth, I cannot say, but
many people believe that Israel either has the bomb or
could produce it very shortly. There is a generator in the
Negev that no foreigner has been allowed to view. It is
also rumored that the Israelis might very well have said to
the Egyptians, "Don't use your rockets." This is only rumor,
and, of course, I cannot verify it; however, the Israeli
soldiers did capture Russian rocket units in Sinai, but the
Egyptians never used them. Whether this is because they
didn't know how, or whether, because of the threat of
the Israelis, no one knows. The story that I heard from
many people in Israel—not from any official member of
Government, but from many who were familiar with high
officials—was to the effect that if Israel had used the
rocket, she would have destroyed Cairo by bombing it.
Further, the Israelis could have blown up the Aswan Dam
and made the Nile River and the Suez Canal radioactive. It
is quite true that the Israelis could have blown up Cairo.
They could have blown up Damascus also, if they had
wanted. They could have taken either Cairo or Damascus
or both cities, but, as they explained to me, neither was
worth taking. They didn't want the cities, they wouldn't
know what to do with them, and why, they pointed out,
should they expose even one Israeli soldier to death for a
vain conquest? They would have considered it immoral
to take a city merely to prove that they could do so; after
the Israelis' spectacular victories, the Arabs knew that they

were capable of taking either one of these capitals, just as they had vanquished Jerusalem.

One of the reasons that gives a ring of truth to this report that the Israeli Government warned Egypt about the use of rockets, is Egypt's use of poison gas in Yemen. If Egypt was capable of this, she was quite capable of using gases of various kinds. For example, she is known to have a nerve gas, one drop of which on the skin of the victim brings paralysis and ultimate death. The Israeli soldiers were aware of this, but they also knew that they could have destroyed the Aswan Dam, and, further, they were cognizant of the fact that had the Arabs been victorious the Israeli cities would have been bombed until there were no buildings left.

Whether the Israeli will regret having been so civilized and limiting their fighting and destruction to the bare minimum is yet to be determined. The Arab world refuses to admit that it has been defeated and talks belligerently of renewing the war.

## NINE

# The Egyptian Dictator

ANTHONY EDEN astutely told President Eisenhower during the Suez crisis of 1956, "Nasser is now effectively in Russian hands just as Mussolini was in Hitler's. It would be as ineffective to placate him as it was to manifest weakness to Mussolini."

How much more pertinent Eden's statement is today! Did Nasser really believe that the Russians loved the Arabs and hated Israel? What the Russians wanted was power. Why did Nasser believe the Russians plied him with three billion dollars' worth of gifts? Surely he did not imagine that the Russians expected nothing in return; largesse of such proportions must be paid for. But Nasser, like all dictators, lost a sense of reality, the ability to be objective. "Power corrupts" is certainly exemplified in this good-looking Egyptian who started out with noble ambitions to lift some of the poverty and economic inequities from the back of the Egyptian peasants. But that didn't seem to be enough for Nasser, and one can't help but get the impression that the pleasure of being in the international limelight got to him. He began to enjoy strutting on the world stage, and to his delight as well as the delight of many Egyptians, he began to be treated seriously. When in a burst of rage he nationalized the Suez Canal and, in spite of pessimistic prophecies, ran it with success, the Arabs were proud. Syria fell into his arms (she didn't stay there long) and has been falling in and out of his arms ever since. He launched the imaginative Aswan Dam, proving that Egypt was losing the race between productive arable land and the expanding population.

But now he is no longer the young reformer whose personal life was simple, even austere. At forty-nine, with his six-foot-two frame and two hundred and twenty pounds, adored by the Egyptians, he might have wrought some great and needed changes in their impoverished economy instead of war and destruction. What weakness sent him into the arms of the Soviets and what fatal flaw drove him to precipitate war against Israel? Did he misjudge the limitations and ability of his own genius, of his army and his generals, or did he rely too much upon the Russians, or did he misjudge them too? A dictator is given one chance by fate; if he muffs it, history takes it away from him.

The Russians are good soldiers only when they are defending Mother Russia, when they are attacked on their own soil. Every time the Russian Army has left Russia to fight an aggressive war, it has faced defeat. It is both the strength and the weakness of the Russians that their military potential comes to aggressive action only when they themselves are attacked.

The strategy the Russian military advisors urged on the Egyptians and Syrians was apparently based on their own topography, their great land masses that enabled them to bleed their invaders by retreating and decoying the invading army farther into the steppes of Russia, far away from their bases.

(If the Germans had read Tolstoy's *War and Peace,* they would have been warned about invading Russia by reviewing the fate of Napoleon.) But the terrain of the Middle East is quite different from that of Russia, and what could work effectively in Russia had no value for the Middle East.

And, while Egypt is a desert, the Egyptian does not live in a desert; he is not oriented to the desert, for he lives in that part of Egypt that is annually inundated and irrigated by the Nile River. It was to increase the area that could be irrigated as the Nile inundates its banks that the Aswan Dam was built. The Egyptian footsoldier on the sands of Sinai was helpless. He fled and died not from wounds but from thirst and exposure to the heat of the day, from the cold of the night.

Where could he fly to? An Israeli flying in an aging Dakota could fly over the Negev and Elath, where so long ago the legendary Queen of Sheba disembarked; over the Dead Sea; over the waters of Galilee, which Jesus walked; over Bethlehem with its shining golden stars; over the green mountains of Syria and Jerusalem the golden. It was all there, packed in a small area over which an Israeli plane could fly a dozen times a day. Russia's land mass gave the Russians space to maneuver; where could the Arabs retreat to—Cairo? Israel could have taken the city had military strategy considered it advisable. Damascus? This too could have been Israel's. What were the Russian military advisors saying to the Arabs when the Israeli armies had them encircled?

What did the war cost? Authoritative estimates figure that the Arabs lost four billion dollars' worth of equipment and installations in the first four days of the war. At a billion dollars a day, this was not only the shortest but also the most expensive war in history. For eleven years the Soviets had poured millions of dollars of military aid into Egypt and Syria. All of it went down the drain in the first forty-eight hours. The United States and Great Britian were losers too, for they had given to Jordan generous military aid which likewise went down the drain.

The Syrians ran from the mountains barefoot to Damascus or were taken prisoner. Syria lost sixty of her hundred aircraft (all of which had been supplied by Russia), plus all of her artillery and most of her tanks. Iraq furnished one brigade and two squadrons and lost them at once. Out of four hundred and fifty aircraft, all supplied by Russia, Egypt lost four hundred and half of her tanks and almost all of her artillery. In addition, she lost tremendous stores of supplies—fuel, food, uniforms, vehicles, ammunition, medicines, and engineering equipment. Also, she lost ships and boats sunk by Israeli frogmen. Egypt forfeited ports, airfields, railways, ordnance workshops, and oil fields, which are now producing $175,000 in oil a day for Israel.

How long will it take Egypt to reconstruct a war machine? At the least a decade, providing Russia continues to supply Egypt as she has in the past. Egypt's economy is sinking. The Egyptian pound sells well below the government quotation. The per capita average income of the Egyptian is ninety-eight dollars a year.

What schools, hospitals, libraries, fertilizer production

these billions of dollars could have meant! And every day since the end of the war, train loads of supplies captured by the Army pour into Israel. The war itself cost the Israeli economy fifty to sixty million dollars and material damage to civilian property estimated at another fifty million dollars. Then, too, there is the expense of keeping their armed forces in the occupied territories and—unlike the Arabs—the Israeli Government will provide pensions to widows and veterans. Premier Levi Eshkol says that because of Egypt's bellicose plans Arab countries and Israel have spent ten billion dollars for war preparations since 1952. What happened to Russian intelligence? Was it unaware of Egypt's weaknesses? The United States secret intelligence must have reported to the United States Government that the *élan* and the discipline of the Israeli army made Israel's victory inevitable. The story was repeated to me many times in Israel—though not authenticated by any official—that American secret intelligence was aware that if the Arabs attacked first it would take the Israelis two or three days to defeat the Arabs but that, on the other hand, if Israel took the first step, she could achieve victory in one day. Russia knew and admitted two hours after the Israeli bombardment of the Egyptian airfields that Egypt was a cooked goose. In this case, the emphasis must be placed on the word goose. What kind of game were the Soviets playing? Could it be possible that they were not as aware as our intelligence was of Israel's superior ability, or were they deliberately, with a sinister intent, leading the Arabs into a quagmire that would have made it easier for the Russians to take over? After all, Russia has hopes of becoming a great power in the Middle East by riding in on the backs of the Arabs.

Surely the Russians must have understood that to ring Israel with armed forces and close the Canal was an act tantamount to a declaration of war and would of necessity bring a firm reaction from Israel. Whether the Israelis fired the first shot, which I am sure they did, was not and is not pertinent. The Arabs were holding a machine-gun at Israel's heart and were about to press the trigger. What was Israel to do—wait until the trigger was pulled? Egypt's act was insane. Nasser seems to have acted stupidly or hysterically and Russia appears to have been lacking in honesty as well as sanity.

The war was spectacular in its brevity and its finality. It was expensive to the pride of Egypt. It displayed Federenko's lying. It caused the United Nations to display its weakness and its ineffectiveness. But the war became something more—an ignominious monument to the lack of just plain common sense on the part of the Russians.

Nasser is more understandable. He had become drunk with his own wine, he had begun to believe his own nonsense: that the Arab countries could survive only if Israel were destroyed; that Arab unity was dependent upon the destruction of Israel. This became his theme song, his litany.

If an individual conducted himself in such an absurd fashion, he would be described as insane. Israel does not have any natural resources; she has no oil, no gold. Land? The Arabs have millions of acres that are uninhabited and not used. Is the Israeli land more valuable than the Arab? It's made of rock and desert, but the Israelis have conquered the land by their sweat and their toil. They knew they had to conquer the desert or the desert would swallow them. What then have the Israelis that the Arabs covet? How can two and a half million people be a menace to a hundred million? Eight thousand square miles is as nothing compared to the vast areas of the Arab world. What nonsense to maintain that Israel is a menace. One would imagine that the Arabs would be too proud to admit that they are afraid of a handful of Jews.

Nasser is too smart not to be cognizant of this fact. What a sick rallying cry with which to divert the impoverished Arab peasant: annihilate the Jews.

Where was the world's sense of humor? Two and a half million people a threat to one hundred million? The idea should have been laughed at and the Arabs should have been told that their attitude was ridiculous and absurd.

## ✵ TEN

# A Handsome King
# Loses His City

IN 1956 I stood outside of the Mandelbaum Gate on the
Israeli side, waiting to find out how the Jordanians were
voting. They were to decide that day whether they were
going to keep the English or throw them out. After the
First World War, the British had carved out of the Otto-
man Empire a piece of land they called Jordan; it became
the Kingdom of Jordan. (The British kept the Jordanian
Kingdom going by giving it thirty-two million dollars
a year. The British trained their soldiers so that the Jordanian army became a famous army of fighting men.)
But nationalism was sweeping through the world and
every little country was intoxicated by the thought of independence.

## Where Were the Arabs?

In any event, on this particular Sunday, after having thrown out the British military men who had been training the Jordanian army, the Jordanians were to vote on whether to retain the British. I did not go into Jordan because the American Consul in Amman told me that if I did go, I couldn't come back, because the Arabs were following the rather uncivilized pattern of not allowing into their country anyone who wanted to go to Israel. (After having been in Egypt, I had been obliged to fly back to the island of Cyprus and travel from there to Israel, instead of going to Israel directly from Egypt.) Barbed wire separated the Israeli section of Jerusalem from the Jordanian. The barbed wire was covered with some Israeli woman's wash, which proved again to me that the stream of life is always stronger and deeper than the stream of death. The Jordanians and the Israelis might be enemies, but—as far as this Israeli woman was concerned—her wash had to dry because she needed the clothes for her children and for her husband and the barbed wire served as an adequate clothesline.

We hung around the Mandelbaum Gate all day; at sundown, word was brought that the Jordanians had voted against the English. I turned to one of my colleagues and said, "Well, it's obvious that they have just committed suicide. How are they going to get along?" I needn't have worried if they threw out the English; the Americans were only too delighted to pick up the check and give them more than the British. And so since 1956 we have given them money, money, money, money. When King Hussein stood before the United Nations and made his eloquent plea, for which he received a standing ovation, it would have been interesting to have figured out how expensive this man really was.

He is quite a handsome chap, not very tall. He has a fine voice, and he spoke with great eloquence, but he costs us a lot of money. Every word he uttered was worth its weight in gold, because we have given Hussein's country five hundred million dollars in the last ten years. A half billion dollars is a heavy burden for the American taxpayer to assume. We could do a lot with that money right here in our own country.

When Hussein spoke he forgot to tell the United Nations that the refugees who were living in such an unhappy plight were the result of the Jordanians fighting the Israelis in 1956. They had been told by their own government that if the Israelis caught them, they would not only kill them, but would also torture them. Of course, there was no truth to that, it was a deliberate falsehood.

A few days before June fifth, using the "hot line" between Jerusalem and Amman, the Israeli Government urged Hussein to stay out of the war, pointing out that there was no reason for the Jordanians and the Israelis to fight, that they certainly could negotiate whatever was necessary. The Israelis were not eager for war, they wanted peace so they might live fruitful years. In my opinion Hussein would have preferred peace, but he also may have been afraid of what would happen to him if he did not acquiesce. When he submitted the question of not going to war, the sheikhs who surround him threw down their guns and said, "Kill us—here are our guns— but do not ask us not to fight the Israelis." So, Hussein went on the Jordanian radio and extorted his soldiers. "Kill the infidel, kill, kill! Kill them with guns, kill them with your hands, kill them with your feet, kill them with your teeth. Kill them, kill them with whatever you have."

Jerusalem was taken house by house; more than a thousand homes were shot and bombed—a bitter fight. An Israeli column followed the first tanks down the street and a squadron of Israeli planes roared across the sky, adding to the attack; the Israeli planes dropped two napalm canisters on Arab positions. All day the fighting went on, men died and men were wounded. In the evening hours, the U.S.-built Patton and Sherman tanks of the Israeli Army moved through the streets into assault positions, hemming in the Arabs, who also had U.S.-built Patton and Sherman tanks. Before the sun rose, Israeli artillery began shelling the Jordanian sector of Jerusalem. The assault would have succeeded much earlier but the Israelis were retarded in their advance because they had been ordered not to use heavy explosives; the Israeli Government was adamant that there be no damage to the holy places, Moslem or Christian.

The Hebrew university on Mount Scopus, closed to the Israelis after the war of 1948, was reclaimed in 1967; the Israeli Army sent as driver of the first bus going up to Mount Scopus the son of the man killed by the Jordanians on his last run to Mount Scopus in 1948. With great sense of historical drama, the son used the same number bus, number nine, his father had been driving when he had been shot.

It was dawn on Wednesday morning, June 6, when an Israeli unit triumphantly passed through the Mandelbaum Gate, no longer in the hands of the Jordanians. They passed around wrecked and gutted tanks and reached the Via Dolorosa, where Jesus had carried His cross on the way to His agony. For eighteen years the Jews had not gone through that gate, but at ten o'clock that morning the flag with the Star of David was raised over the golden dome of the famous Mosque of Omar. History stood still at that moment for a new day had dawned, and a new event occurred in the history of mankind. To make the capitulation complete, almost immediately after the Israeli flag had been raised in the morning skies over the golden dome, an entourage of Jordanians arrived, including the Arab governor of the city, a Moslem religious judge and other officials, who assured the Israeli commander that there would be no more shooting.

Then the Senior Chaplain of the Israeli Army, General Goren, his battle ribbons across his chest from the preceding two wars, stood before the few remaining stones of the Temple of Solomon, known as the Wailing Wall, and with a trembling voice and tears running down his cheeks, uttered the sacred prayer: "Praise the Lord. Trust in the Lord Israel, for He is Thy strength and Thy shield. He has heard Thy supplication. He has become Thy salvation."

For the first time in more than nineteen hundred years, the flag with the Star of David flew over Jerusalem. It had not done so since the Roman general Titus had marched his legions into the Temple to find the mysterious God of the Jews, whom they worshiped and for whose sake they refused to bow to the Roman gods—a refusal that meant death for them. He would find their God, destroy him, and prove to the Jews that He was impotent in the face of Roman power. So, Titus and his legions marched into the Temple, down to the Holy of the Holies, and tore the drapes aside from the shrine but here he found no image of a god that could be broken into pieces or destroyed, only the Laws given to the Jews through Moses—the Ten Commandments. This was their God, the Moral Law; so it had been through the ages. Man, the Moral Law taught, must regulate his relationship with man by his relationship with God. Not since that day had Jerusalem been theirs, and on this June day in 1967 there flooded through the land an emotion difficult to comprehend, one of spiritual exaltation as well as military pride. Other victories against the Arabs were a necessary achievement for survival, but Jerusalem was different; this was more than survival, this was a spiritual experience, a victory exalted beyond military victory. No sooner had the gates opened than a hundred thousand people, as if animated by the same impulse, walked the long uphill path to the Wailing Wall. Strong men wept, soldiers and civilians alike. General Goren exulted: "Now we take an oath that we will never leave this place. The Wailing Wall belongs to us. This Holy place was our God's place; from here we do not move—never, never."

The Arabs in the Jordanian portion of Jerusalem fled, then tried to return some days later when they discovered that the Jews did not want their houses or possessions. White flags made of sheets or pillow cases were placed outside their windows or doors; this was enough to keep them safe. There was no looting, no raping. The Mayor of Hebron, a Jordanian city, expressed his appreciation for the orderly way the Jews took over. I could see the Arabs streaming back with their few possessions—pots and pans, and here and there a donkey.

But who can explain the ecstatic thrill that ran throughout Israel when the news came that Jerusalem had been taken? For eighteen years the Israelis had not been allowed in the Old City, but now, the Mandelbaum Gate barrier was broken down and Israeli soldiers poured through. Who can describe the indescribable feeling that swept over Israel when the Chief Rabbi of the Israeli Army announced, "Jerusalem is ours. Jerusalem the Golden is ours!"

One can understand the reactions of the Orthodox—some of them almost bigoted in their Orthodoxy; but why should a sophisticated people, many of them quite irreligious, have been swept by the same impulse to go to the Wailing Wall and stand before the remnants of the Temple of Solomon?

To reach the Wailing Wall, you must traverse a road that winds up a steep hill. There is no way of getting there by car and the walk is nearly a mile under a blazing sun, and a mile to return. Yet, thousands began the climb.

Soldiers—tough, hard-looking men—wept as they stood there and prayed. There is a custom, observed in the past by Orthodox Jews praying at the Wailing Wall, to leave a note addressed directly to God. I spoke to one of the professors at the university and asked him if he had gone to the Wailing Wall. "Yes," he replied. "Why?" I asked. "You're not a believer." "That is true," he said. "I am not a believer, but I went because if my mother and father had been living, they would have gone." "Did you leave a note to God?" "Certainly." A little puzzled, I asked, "Do you mind very much telling me what you wrote to God?" "I don't mind at all," he said. "It was not a private conversation. I wrote, *'Dear God, let there be peace in the world.'* "

# ✸ ELEVEN

# The Voice in the Blood

THE DÉCOR of many of the Hilton Hotels is predictable. The lobbies and the Coca-Cola are, in a sense, a transplanted bit of America. I've gotten so that I can identify the rugs in the lobbies; they are generally two solid colors—some purple and gray, some green and blue. I have seen them in West Berlin, in Istanbul, in Hong Kong—wherever I have encountered a Hilton Hotel. I experience a friendly, warm feeling at the sight of the familiar rugs.

The Hilton Hotel in Tel Aviv is quite handsome, particularly the magnificent carved doors leading to the dining room. Every room has a balcony that looks out onto the Mediterranean. Having breakfast on the balcony, listening to the pounding of the waves and observing some of the early-morning risers swimming in that sea of blue and green where so much of history has taken place is one of the pleasures I look forward to.

I was in Tel Aviv late in September 1966, and just as I was checking out, I noticed in the art gallery located in the lobby a canvas that immediately caught my fancy. I went over at once and examined it with excitement; the canvas was a huge one covered with enormous impressionistic roses. Unfortunately I had no time to inquire about the canvas since I was already late in leaving to catch my plane for New York. But in June 1967, when the hotel was almost empty, I was waiting in the lobby for Al Rosen (we were going to Syria) when I suddenly remembered the canvas. I walked back to the gallery, wondering if the canvas was still there. A woman was sitting at the desk—very attractive, about forty-five, with copper hair. When she looked up questioningly, I said, "When I was here in September, I saw a canvas," and I began to describe it to her. "I just wondered if it was still here."

"Madame, you have just described the finest painting we have in our collection. Would you like to see it again?" She took me back to the display where once more I saw the striking canvas. It was painted by Moshe Katz, one of the finest contemporary Israeli painters.

How can one tell why a particular painting will move one? It seems as inexplicable as why certain people attract us. Where people are concerned it's said to be chemistry, but that does not explain the fascination of a certain canvas. I remember the first time I saw Raphael's *Madonna* in Dresden. It was hanging against black velvet with a red cord securing it so that no viewer could touch it. I trembled with excitement at the beauty of the painting. Today it is not considered sophisticated to be enthusiastic about

Raphael; he painted beautiful women and—even worse than painting intoxicatingly beautiful faces—his subjects can be identified. But he communicates with me and brings me much pleasure. I had the same such feeling about this canvas. It was a large one and the roses almost gigantic. I could almost feel the pricking of the thorns, even though the painting was impressionistic rather than realistic. I stared and stared and said at last to the copper-haired woman: "What does that painting sell for?"

"Twelve thousand five hundred dollars," she answered.

"Well," I said wistfully, "take off the twelve and I'll buy it." Even that would have meant hocking my winter outfit, but it would have been worth the price, for I could not take my eyes off it. I loved that painting.

The handsome woman owned the gallery. She was urbane and delightful and I would have liked to spend more time with her. The conversation naturally turned to the war and particularly the taking of Jerusalem. I was curious about her explanation of the almost mystical Jewish reaction to the city's capture.

"Can you tell me why all this emotion about the Wailing Wall? Why is everyone going there? What is it that compels them?" She reflected for a moment, then answered, "I came here from Switzerland some fifteen years ago with my husband, from whom I am now divorced. He is a real hypochondriac. He wouldn't walk half a block for fear he would injure his heart, and he is not what you would call a religious man. Yet that man, who has not walked more than a block in years, that man walked the full length to the Wailing Wall and back!" We were interrupted momentarily by her daughter, who was about eighteen, dressed in a very short skirt and looking like any attractive American college girl of the same age. After she walked away, the woman turned to me and said, "You saw my daughter? Have you ever seen anyone more modern in appearance than that?"

I shook my head. "You see," she continued, "it's not only in appearance that she's modern, but in her thinking she is a true contemporary. Yet that daugher of mine—who isn't religious, who won't go anywhere if she can't go in a car —took a bus, stood all the way, and rode up to Jerusalem, forty miles away, so she could walk up the hill to the Wailing Wall." There was silence between us for a moment.

"How do you account for that?" I asked. She pondered for a little before answering, then said with great penetration, "You know, it's a voice in the blood that talks to all of us."

A *voice in the blood,* I said to myself. I wondered, and yet I knew that Israel was full of people reacting in the same way. A voice in the blood calling through millenia of time. The owner of that art gallery had with great wisdom illuminated for me the whole emotional reaction of Israel to the taking of Jerusalem.

Earlier that day, I had met in the hotel elevator a middle-aged woman who asked me if I knew how soon the plane flights would be resumed and when the United States Government would allow people to come to Israel. In the conversation that ensued, she explained to me that she was waiting for her son. "Oh," I asked, "you must be visiting here?" "No," she answered. "I live here in Israel, but I am here at the hotel during the war." "How do you happen to be living in Israel?" I asked. "Oh, its a long story and would probably not interest you." "Of course it would," I assured her. "Let's have a cup of coffee together. I've got a half-hour and it would be interesting to know how you came here." She looked like any American clubwoman; her hair was properly done, her shoes stylish, and her rings were rather opulent.

## Where Were the Arabs?

At the table she started her story. "I was born in Russia. My parents went to the United States when I was about two years old. That was 72 years ago. We loved America. My father kissed the ground of the United States when we landed there, because we were free. My father worked sixteen hours a day. My brothers worked. I worked when I was twelve."

"Where was that?" I asked.

"We all worked in a silk factory in New Jersey (that was before rayon and nylon). I worked for ten hours a day. Every hour was an hour of labor that we loved because we were free. We no longer had fears. We were Jews, but we could be free. We could own property, we could own money, we could go to temple, we could do anything we desired.

"We felt that we were part of the great land of America where other people were free to do as they pleased. In due time, we prospered. All the children brought their money home. All pooled together. We gave it to our father and he bought property and we continued to prosper."

She had married at twenty-three and, eventually, had three sons. Her sons went to college and she said, "I took private lessons in English so they shouldn't be ashamed of me when their friends came to the house.

"But you know," she said "the Friday of the week in which President Truman recognized the State of Israel, I came to a decision. My husband had died two years before and, suddenly I wanted to go to Israel. I told my sons about it. They thought I was foolish. What did I need to go there for? Why couldn't I stay home with all of my friends and family? But how could I explain to them what it was that moved me? I wanted at last to belong to a majority. I wanted to come where I felt I belonged."

In any event, she came to Israel and had been there ever since. She was very businesslike and apparently had taken

74

what money she had and invested it. She bought an apartment building and lived in one of the flats; on the money she received in rent from the other units, she was able to pay her expenses. Periodically her sons urged her to return to the United States, but she steadfastly refused. When they found she was quite content, they stopped urging her to return; she was even able to persuade one of the sons to put some money into an Israeli business.

She had left her flat (which had been sandbagged for protection against the bombing, as were many of the buildings in Tel Aviv) and registered at the hotel, where she felt safer. She had expected her son that week but there were no planes flying; she had not heard from him and she had been unable to reach him. Telephone calls were reportedly taking one month to place; thousands of people were waiting to get a line. I told her not to worry; I was sure that within one week the plane service would be restored. I also offered to telephone her son when I landed in New York—he lived in Trenton. (When I did phone him, he thanked me profusely and told me he had stopped urging his mother to come back to the United States when she appeared happy in Israel—but "that doesn't keep her from worrying about her sons, so we take turns every three or four months and fly over to see her.")

I could not help but reflect on how strange an incident this was. In an elevator at the Hilton in Tel Aviv, during a war, I meet a woman who was born in Russia, came to the United States as an infant, and married and prospered, but found ultimately that she could find peace only in Israel.

I asked her if she had been to the Wailing Wall. "Yes, I've been to the Wailing Wall." "And what did you do there?" "I cried. I cried because my parents are dead, I cried because my husband is dead, I cried because I love my children so much and worry because something might happen to them, but mostly I cried for all of the mothers whose sons could never come to the Wailing Wall because they were killed fighting the Arabs."

*The Jerusalem Post* on Monday, June 19, carried an excerpt from *In the Heart of the Seas* by Jerusalem's Nobel laureate, S. Y. Agnon, in which he recites some of the tradition and legend about the Wailing Wall:

> The Western Wall, the vestige of our treasures of ancient days, which the Almighty in His mercy left for us, is the height of twelve people symbolizing the Twelve Tribes. This is so that each Jew should direct his thoughts according to his own height, at his stone. No structure in the world has such stones, without any kind of plaster holding them together, yet they hold together, like the Jewish people, which has no government to hold it together, yet is one united entity.
>
> We are told that the Wall's foundation row consists of seven stones, laid by Adam, Abraham, Isaac, Jacob, Joseph, David and Solomon.
>
> When Solomon set about building the Temple, he summoned assemblies of the entire nation and cast lots for the labor. The construction of the Western Wall fell to the poor, working class. The wealthier classes hired others to do their work for them. The poor, however, built their section by their own toil. When the holy work was ended, the Shekhina [Divine Presence] descended and rested on the Western Wall, saying: "The toil of the poor is precious in My eyes and My blessing shall be upon it." Then a Heavenly Voice added: "The Divine Presence shall never be removed from the Western Wall."
>
> When the Temple was destroyed and the other three walls had fallen, a Roman general came to demolish the Western Wall—and he dropped dead on the spot. Another general came—and all his limbs withered. Then came Titus himself, and a

Heavenly Voice spoke up: "O wicked son of a wicked man! Turn back, do not approach! All the walls have I given over to you except this one!" But Titus ignored the voice and raised his sledge-hammer to start breaking the Wall—and his right hand withered.

Just then, six Angels descended from Heaven, seated themselves atop the Wall and wept. Their tears seeped into the Wall, mingled with the stones, and hardened into a cement that holds the Wall together forever.

Over the centuries, the Western Wall, like the rest of Mount Moriah [the Temple Mount] and much of the rest of Biblical Jerusalem, was buried under rubble and rubbish. Its rediscovery is variously credited to the Caliph Omar, Sultan Suleiman and Sultan Selim—the last in about 1560. One day, when Selim was in Jerusalem, he saw an old woman bringing a mass of dung and garbage and dumping it on a spot near his palace. Angrily he had the woman brought before him. The woman said she was a "Roman" [Christian], and that the bishops had ordered Christians to dump garbage on the spot where the Temple had stood, so that it would be swamped and forgotten. He investigated and found that she had spoken the truth. So he had many coins of gold and silver buried in different parts of the mountain of rubbish, and issued a proclamation calling on the poor to come and dig up the money. More than 10,000 men worked for 30 days till the dunghill was cleared and the Western Wall stood revealed as it is seen today. Selim then issued a strict prohibition against the practice of dumping garbage or spitting in the area, or in any other way desecrating the Holy Mountain.

So the wall stood through the centuries waiting for the Jews to return.

# TWELVE

# In the Lovely Month of May

ONE EVENING around eight o'clock, tired and thirsty after our trip to Sinai, Al and I went into the cocktail lounge at the Tel Aviv Hilton. The place was packed with correspondents from all over the world; you sat anywhere there was an available chair, and there was no such thing as a private table. I had difficulty adjusting to what was reality—the Sinai Desert, where we had seen millions of dollars' worth of hardware left by the fleeing Egyptians and dead bodies of Arabs in grotesque grimaces without the serenity of a peaceful death, or this crowded bar with a flow of conversation, every correspondent with a different story of what he had seen.

I found myself sitting next to M. No introductions were necessary; we just sat and joined in the conversation. For four hours we listened to this particularly articulate Israeli, who went over the steps leading to the war. We drank whiskey sours, we ate peanuts; we drank more whiskey sours, ate more peanuts, and still he talked on. He did stop once, to call his wife. (I overheard his conversation: she must have asked him what he was doing. "Talking and drinking," he said. Then she must have asked him what he was going to do, because he answered, "Talk and drink some more.") A little while later his wife joined us; we left the bar and went to the restaurant below, and still he talked. By then the crowd had increased to about eighteen.

M was a big man, probably over 6'2". It was as though his inner being were aflame, but he knew the story of the war and the weeks that preceded it. "In the lovely month of May," he said with emotion, "when the tender greens prepared for the deeper and richer hues of June, a horrified world watched a unique unification of the Arab world for the purpose of erasing Israel from the world and from history. King Hussein forgot, or decided to ignore, the insults hurled at him for months by Egypt; he journeyed to Cairo, embraced Nasser, kissed him, and vowed eternal brotherhood. The embrace was witnessed and applauded by Ahmed Shukairy of the Palestinian organization.

"While lilacs bloomed and blossomed and withered away in your country," he said, turning to me, "King Feisal of Saudi Arabia, known as a friend to the West and suspicious of Nasser, nevertheless dismissed his doubts and sent twenty thousand soldiers into Jordan. While the wild mustard and lavender thistle covered the meadows in Syria and the valleys in Israel, an Iraqui unit joined the Egyptian soldiers poised in Sinai; while other Iraqui troops joined up with the Syrian troops, Kuwait flew an infantry brigade into Egypt. They were busy, those Arab countries. Sudan flew an infantry brigade into Egypt and stopped growing cotton; Libya joined the parade and dispatched infantrymen into Sinai.

"When May slipped into June, and your roses burst into magnificence as I have seen them do in your country, the Western world was hypnotized into inactivity. They listened with almost stupified horror to Nasser boasting in a radio broadcast, 'The armies of all the Arab nations, Algeria, Kuwait, the Sudan, Iraq, are behind us.' For the Israelis flowers bloomed too, but who could say they would not become a funeral wreath for all of Israel?

"But wait," he said as he ordered another drink. "The plot is just beginning to unfold. On the morning of June fifth, when the dawning sky was streaked with orange and gold, that sky which had looked down upon Jacob and Abraham and David and Jesus and Peter, that sky was suddenly alive with Israeli army planes: all that they had were in the sky; only twelve were left behind to defend Israel. With deadly accuracy these young Israeli pilots struck not only the planes but the radar and antiaircraft sites at the big Abu Suweir airbase near Ismalia on the western bank of the Suez. It's difficult to believe this, but the Egyptian Mig pilots were drinking coffee when the Israeli jets streaked in and blasted the interceptors lined up on the runway—no one seems to know whether it was even operational. These Israeli pilots flew to the bases at El 'Arîsh and Bir Gifgafa in north Sinai and destroyed them. They annihilated targets at El Shatt, Ras Sudr, El Tor, and Ras Umm Sidd on the west and south. These young pilots wasted no ammunition: every bomb counted. They were economical with their weapons, precise in their aim, cool in their behavior.

"They had with them, as I told you before, the entire armada of the Israeli air force—only twelve planes were left behind for the defense of their land. They could afford no mistakes and they made none." This impassioned

Israeli stood up and walked away from the table for a moment; he was obviously deeply moved, and those of us who listened were spellbound by his eloquence and feeling.

"They had to immobilize the enemy; they had vowed that the Mediterranean would not be red with their blood as the Arabs had prophesied; their children and their wives were hostages to their determination. They guided their planes neither for glory nor for vengeance, but for the life of their nation." He toyed with his glass for a moment, then turned to us and said, "Do you understand this? You who came to report this war so strange in every way, do you know what was at stake? Our lives—all of our lives."

The speaker sagged; fatigue was overcoming him. His wife told us he had not slept in thirty-six hours. We ordered him another drink. "No, no," he said, "I don't want another drink. I'm going home, for the end of the story is here. You see, they had only one choice—success or death—and on that morning the Israeli fliers, the young fliers, the bronzed airmen of Israel, established their reputation as unerring marksmen for ages to come. They became legendary."

He rose and said, "Thank you for listening."

There was nothing more to be said; the group dispersed and our Israeli went home to sleep at last. I was so tired and emotionally spent after listening for those many hours I couldn't fit my key into the keyhole. Al Rosen came to my rescue; from his room he had heard me fumbling with the doorknob. I parted the drapes and walked onto the balcony. There, under the silver light of the moon, the moon men soon hoped to conquer, I watched the Mediterranean move in its restless rhythm and heard its thundering noise and wondered if, somewhere in the heavens, someone did not sing: *Let peace shine like a benediction on the faces of men.*

## THIRTEEN

# A Celebration Party in Jerusalem

I HAD BEEN INVITED to a celebration party given by Professor F. My car drove me up to an apartment building (there are few villas in Israel, land is too valuable and expensive). To enter a building in Jerusalem, which is built on hills, generally means walking up quite a flight of steps. Under the white moonlight so characteristic of Jerusalem the buildings were clearly discernible. My host and his wife greeted me with great cordiality, but that was the last I saw of them. The apartment was crowded and everyone seemed to know each other; they were old friends come together to share their war experiences. Some were absent because of the loss of a son or husband—death had touched many households. I was given a drink, introduced to a number of people, and then I wandered around listening to the conversations.

Mrs. B was reciting her experience. She lives in a house on the outermost street of the Israeli portion of Jerusalem, contiguous to the Jordanian part. "Why did you live so close to the Arab sector?" I asked her. "Because, I was crazy about the house—I could do things with it, and I had it made over. Also, it has a beautiful view. You must come and see it. I was in the garage when the shooting started, and I don't mind telling you I was frightened. I wanted to get into the house so I could turn on the radio and find out what was really happening, but the shooting continued and I was afraid to run through the breezeway to the house for fear I would be caught in the firing. So I crawled on my stomach into the living room, but just then the windows in the living room were blown out and with great speed I reversed my crawl and went back to the garage.

"I sat huddled on the floor, not knowing how close the Arabs were. There was a lull in the bombing. I couldn't endure it any longer; sitting there in the garage was like waiting to be executed. So without any prudence or good sense, I got into my car and drove out onto the street. I was going to a friend of mine who lived in an apartment, to see if there was room in the shelter. I realize now it was a wild thing to do, because a bullet went through one of my tires. I jumped out of the car, which careened on to the curb, and I ran as I have never run until I reached an apartment house where I stayed in the hallway until the morning."

"Did you get back to your house?" I asked. "Oh, yes— yesterday; but what a mess it was! The Arabs had cut the electric wires and my refrigerator had stopped functioning. The butter had melted and the fish had begun to smell. I never want to see fish again. I will have to go out and do some shopping tomorrow because the electricity is going to be restored." I stared at her; she was elegantly dressed and her hair was teased into a stylish hairdo. She had jewels on her fingers. But she told her story as though it was an everyday occurrence to have her house bombed and her car shot out from under her.

"What was the first thing you did," I asked her, "when you finally got home?" "I called my beauty shop, then my friends to see if they were all right, and then I started cleaning the kitchen."

A red-haired woman spoke up. "All I've done since mobilization is wash diapers!" She turned to me: "My diaper man is in the army." I must have looked incredulous. She laughed and explained: "I have a two-year-old and a one-year-old and I'm taking care of my sister's two children, who are one-year-old twins, while she's in the hospital having another baby; that's why I need so many diapers."

Another guest chimed in. "I'm convinced the halo of maternity is a diaper."

"Oh, come," I said, "with a war on, diapers do not seem so important."

"Well," remarked the mother of two and the keeper of two others, "one diaper may not seem too significant, but dozens are more formidable than the Arabs."

"Well, they both smell alike," another guest ventured.

I caught snatches of other conversations. "Yes, I took my daughter-in-law to the hospital. Wouldn't you know it, she has to have an acute appendectomy when the Jordanians attack the hospital; my daughter-in-law does everything the hard way, but in a dramatic fashion. Yes, yes, she's all right. I don't worry about her, I've got three sons in Sinai."

The editor of *The Jerusalem Post* arrived, an American who had come to Israel some years before, fell in love with it, and decided to stay. The editions printed during the week of June fifth had already become collectors' items. The paper carried many personal items which are read with universal interest. Gossip columns are popular because people are naturally gossips, a perfectly legitimate trait. We all love to hear intimate things about the people we know or those we know about. This is a universal characteristic shared by Americans, Israelis, and even the Russians—though they don't learn as much about their public officials as we do. So far we have managed to learn that Stalin was irrationally cruel, Khrushchev had bad manners, and that Kosygin and company blundered in the Middle East.

One item that roused great interest in *The Jerusalem Post* was the notice a couple inserted in the paper stating that they were about to get a divorce but they had now decided to remain together to strengthen the unity of Israel.

I wandered over to another group and was introduced to Judge Landau, who had presided over the Eichmann trial. One of the group turned to me and said, "As an American and a correspondent, what do you think was responsible for the rapid defeat of the Arabs?" Before I had a chance to answer, one of the other guests said, "Our soldiers fought with tenacity and grim intensity because they had the memory of the Nazis and their savagery." I ventured, "In another generation, the young Israelis will no longer have that same iron courage, for neither they nor their parents will have lived through the Nazi concentration camps." It was then that Judge Landau spoke up. "I don't believe," he said, "our younger generation will forget. During the Eichmann trial, the evidence was piped into the schoolrooms. They are not likely to forget that story." Judge Landau has a noble face, and it must have been a grueling task to preside over the terrible trial. Judge Landau presided with the most meticulous regard for the law and all the benefits allowed by that law to an accused prisoner were accorded Eichmann. There are no jury trials in Israel. A panel of judges listens to the evidence in murder trials, and reaches the verdict.

One voice roused my attention. The speaker was a slim, dark man somewhere between fifty and sixty. I heard him say, "What do the Americans really know about the travail of Israel? It's easy to send money."

"Oh, come on now," I broke in, "why do you deprecate the gifts of money sent by the Americans?"

He looked at me sharply. "Are you an American? I thought you were a Sabra."

I laughed, "Yes, I know. A Sabra is a cactus fruit, prickly on the outside but sweet on the inside. I wouldn't mind being a Sabra. I am sure you must be one."

"No, I'm not," he answered. "Let's declare a truce and let me explain why I said to give money is good but Americans really do not know how brutal or hard it's been; how we had to fight against every possible odds." Coffee was brought in at that moment and someone whispered to me, "He just lost his nephew, a flier."

"First," I said, "before you explain your deep feelings, would you let me know where you come from?"

"Sure," he said. "My three brothers and I came from Russia, but let me be more explicit." His intensity was such that he commanded the attention of everyone in the room. "Do you know what the British were like after the Balfour Declaration? The League of Nations assigned their mandate for Palestine to Great Britain. The Balfour pledge publicly recognized the historical connection of the Jewish people with Palestine and granted to them the right to build their national home in Palestine. Great Britain was specifically instructed to facilitate emigration and to encourage settlement of Jews on the land.

"Do you know how they executed this order? By nefariously betraying us. The Arabs began to riot when the Jews began to arrive, although they had sold the land to the Jews. Great Britain, who is a two-faced Janus, instead of encouraging immigration began to woo the Arabs. She had an economic interest and military bases in the Arab countries. Besides she cynically recognized that there are more Arabs than Jews. Didn't her present foreign minister, Mr. Brown, say the same thing only a few days ago? In any event, she issued a so-called White Paper in 1939 limiting the number of emigrants into Palestine to fifteen thousand a year for five years, and after that no more until the Arabs approved. You will notice that the British gave the Arabs every advantage." He kept stirring his coffee violently but did not drink any. He was showing his disdain and hatred for the English as he stirred his coffee.

"It was during these years," he continued, "that ship after ship was turned away from Palestine. Ships loaded with Jewish refugees who had no other place to go, if they could not get into Palestine, but the gas chambers."

Someone interrupted: "Uris told about it in his famous book, *Exodus*."

The dark man waited for a moment, then continued. "The Jews were bitter. Were they supposed to clap their hands and say 'goody, goody' to the English? President Truman requested the British to allow a hundred thousand refugees into Palestine, but the British refused. So we organized the Haganah, the Stern Gang, the Irgun, political armies and terrorists. They functioned; we gave the British a jolly bad time. In 1947, the General Assembly requested Great Britain to leave within eight months. During these eight months, the British officers in Pales-

tine showed their spite. They could have easily maintained
order, instead of which they closed their eyes to Arab
bands who roamed the country murdering, robbing, and
attacking convoys en route to Jewish settlements. The
Arabs would kill the drivers and the passengers. Britain
even carried her spite to such an extent that, weeks before
they left, the British communication workers were ordered
to dismantle parts of the cable and the wireless systems
and telephone wire. But all things come to an end, even
the British, who announced that they would leave at midnight on May 14, which happened to be a Friday. Ben-
Gurion issued a statement saying that the moment the
British left, a Jewish State would be declared.

"We had other troubles besides the British. We have the
Orthodox, who are quite fanatic, and since for them the
Jewish Sabbath begins at sunset, it meant that no religious
Jew would sign his name or ride in an automobile on the
Sabbath. So Ben-Gurion would have to get the official document declaring Israel a State before sunset on Friday or
the Orthodox Jew wouldn't attend the ceremony. But this
was a small problem; secret invitations were sent out to
some two hundred Palestinian Jews. They were told to
wear festive clothes. The time and place were kept secret
so the British wouldn't find out. A few moments after four
o'clock on the afternoon of May 14, before the sun set, the
Israeli Philharmonic Orchestra played what was to become
the national anthem and Ben-Gurion took exactly seventeen minutes to read the nine-hundred-seventy-nine-word
document which declared the independence of the State of
Israel."

"Were you there?" I asked.

"Yes, I was, and I don't mind telling you, I and many
of the other men there wept."

He moved from his chair to the couch. The room was
silent; everyone was listening. Many of them had lived

through that period. "So," he said, "what happened the next day? The Egyptians bombed Tel Aviv, and in Cairo the secretary-general of the Arab League spoke like a true Arab, brutally and boastfully, 'There will be a wave of extermination and a murderous massacre. We will kill the Jews.' "

"What did you do then?" I asked.

"We did what we have always done. We defeated them and we lived. Tell me, you American," he said, "how can money equal the bloodshed of these days? You see my hands. They are tough and hard from breaking stones; that's how we built our State. Then, in 1956, we faced the Arabs again—every ten years they have to have a blood-letting. We defeated them, but once more many of us died. To give money is easy by comparison. Why didn't you come here and build and fight as we did?"

"When did you come to Israel?" I asked, without answering his question.

"I came here from Russia with my three brothers—I told you that. We went to Turkey and then we walked here, all four of us. Do you know how many are left? Only I. My youngest brother was shot by the British in 1940. My other two brothers were killed by the Arabs in the war of 1948. Two days ago, my nephew died in Sinai. He was a flier. How much money is that worth? A million dollars each for my brothers and my nephew!" I could understand his bitterness but I could also see his grief was coloring his judgment.

One of his friends said, "Don't judge him too harshly, his grief is raw and he is lashing out. You see, he brought up this nephew, after his brother was killed, as though he were his own son." I went over to the Israeli, who was still stirring his coffee. He looked up at me with a wry smile and said, "Nu, did I hurt your feelings?" "Yes," I answered, "but not because of what you said about American money, but because of your grief, because I, too, have known what it is to have the angel of death pass over my door because of war and I weep with you in your sorrow."

It is true that much American and European money has flowed into Israel. By May 1967, hundreds of millions of dollars of Israeli bonds had been purchased by Americans. The Israeli Government has never defaulted on the interest or redemption of the bonds. Thirty new cities have been built in Israel; a hundred million trees have been planted. To fly over the Middle East and see the craggy, barren hills from where the soil has been eroded through the centuries and then to see the hills covered with the green of a hundred million trees is a thrilling sight. And each year the Israeli Government proposes to plant six million tree, one in memory of each Jew killed by the Nazis. The trees are noble monuments, and for the Israelis a symbol also that the roots of their national life are embedded forever in this land.

The money has been used to build factories, chemical plants, museums, art galleries, a zoo, universities, new agricultural products, and so on. In a little country— less than eight thousand square miles—you can find practically everything being produced or manufactured.

For example, the city of Ashdod was started seven years ago. It was raised on the sand dunes alone: no arable land was used for its site. It was intended for and is now functioning as a supplementary harbor to Tel Aviv to take care of the loading and unloading of ships. In seven years, these sand dunes have been turned into a lovely city, and the harbor will ultimately accommodate twenty-five ships. There is a great lighthouse with a tremendous beacon. There are apartment houses built of white stone and a few villas, a medical center, maternity center, a theater, a shopping center, schools, factories. All this was barren only seven years ago; today there are bushes, trees, streets beautifully paved and clean. I was dressed in a white dress and never got a spot on it, so clean is the city the Israelis have built out of the desert.

It must be noted that the Arabs who live in Israel, who have been taught to cultivate the land, have gone to school, receive the same prices for their produce as do the Israeli farmers, and have had advice from Israeli agronomists can produce as well as the Israelis. This merely proves that the Arab, if he has an opportunity, can and will take advantage of it like everyone else. He's lived in this impoverished and bleak fashion for centuries. There's nothing the matter with the ability of the Arabs—they have just had no opportunity.

Water was available only a couple of hours a day in the Jordanian part of Jerusalem. How can you stay clean if there is no water? The first thing the Israeli Government did when it annexed the old part of Jerusalem, was to make water available twenty-four hours a day. The same sanitation and the same health conditions now will exist there which have existed in Israeli Jerusalem, and such conditions plus the availability of water will doubtless do much to improve the well-being of the Jordanians.

Much American money (private, not government funds) has been given to Israel to develop the country. One has to see it to realize what a miracle they have produced. But why do not the fabulously wealthy Arabs give their money for the purpose of building up their land as the Israelis have? The wealth of the Arab oil countries is awesome. It is reported that the Sheikh of Kuwait and King Feisal of Saudi Arabia have between them a billion and a half dollars stacked away in British banks. No one knows how much they have in Swiss banks. Why don't they take this money and use it for the development of their land? Why don't they irrigate? Why don't they make it green and verdant as the Israelis have? They have the money.

## Where Were the Arabs?

Last year King Feisal's income from oil was eight hundred million dollars. This year it would have been a billion if the Arabs had not boycotted oil sales to the Western nations. As a result of the boycott they lost three hundred thousand dollars a day. (A rather expensive peeve for them. In the meanwhile the West has been able to procure all the oil it needs from other sources.)

Why should the per capita income of Israel be around fifteen hundred dollars a year, Egypt only ninety-eight dollars, and the other Arab countries even less? Why don't the wealthy Arabs build their countries into green oases to become a challenge to the Israelis? How many Rolls-Royces, how many yachts, how many planes, how many wives can they use? They have occupied these lands for millennia; the peasants live and suffer and are as disease-ridden as they were centuries ago. If they stopped their fanatic conviction that they must destroy Israel, they could, in association, increase their trade, profit from Israeli know-how, and take advantage of Israeli medical knowledge. Even now, the Jordanians surreptitiously cross through the Mandelbaum Gate with military passes to get into an Israeli hospital. I can only explain the Arabs' insanity about destroying Israel, which has sent them to war three times so disastrously, by quoting Dostoevski's belief that "man is irrational and his own worst enemy."

# ✵ FOURTEEN

# The Mountains of Syria

WE FLEW to the border of Syria, the country from whose action the Israelis had suffered the most. From their high hills the Syrians would snipe at the schools and settlements below. Israeli settlers were in constant danger, although the 1956 armistice had outlawed such shooting. It was not much at a time—one man killed, one house bombed, a small group assaulted, but when it was added up through the years, it became a constant irritant, and a danger. There were more than a hundred thousand complaints presented to the United Nations commission, but nothing resulted. Now the Israelis, with cool contempt, decided to take care of Syria. First they had destroyed Egypt; then they took Jordan, the Sinai

Peninsula, the Gaza Strip. Now it was the Syrians' time to face Israeli vengeance.

For two decades the Syrians had engaged in raids on the Israel border settlements. So frequent were these raids that even the children had learned to go into the shelters as a matter of course. For the first three days of the week of June fifth, children of the Kibbutz Don and the Harvest Hill Kibbutz as well as others were in the shelters while the Syrian guns plastered and wrecked the crops ready for harvest. In one of the settlements, all the able-bodied men were in the Army; only five were left in the kibbutz. An apple specialist took charge of the defense. A machine gun was in the living room of one of the houses. Because the inhabitants had been drilled to find refuge in the shelters, there was no panic. The cows were milked as always and when the shelling destroyed electrical power, the people sat in their shelters by candlelight. There were bunks for the babies, first-aid kits, and food in the shelters.

By Thursday, the fourth day, more than half of the buildings had been destroyed in some of these settlements. Crops, trees, plants, buildings, farm machinery were destroyed to the tune of millions of dollars for the four days the settlements had taken a beating from the Syrian shelling. Then the Israeli Army, having laid low the other Arab countries, turned to avenge the destruction and harassment inflicted by the Syrians through the years. Determined to wrest the high ground from the Syrians and once and for all give the Israeli settlements in the plains security, the Israeli Army launched a methodical yard-by-yard artillery bombardment on the tier of trenches and gun emplacements in the mountains.

The Syrian hills were tunneled to a depth of seventy feet in order to accommodate the howitzers; the tunnels were loaded with armament and food. The fortifications extended for a depth of five miles. Flying over these mountains, one could only judge these hills to be impregnable. Not so for the Israelis, for after the artillery bombardment Israeli ground forces began a bloody mop-up operation. For hours the hills echoed with the detonation of demolition charges. The Syrians were now face-to-face with an army; it was no longer a sniping attack on settlements below from their mountain position. This kind of fighting the Syrians could not face; they fled. Israeli soldiers found that the Syrians had retreated so rapidly and had abandoned their trucks and tanks so fast that the ignition keys were still in place.

The Israelis did not win their victory over the Syrians without some cost. Two of their pilots were taken and executed in Damascus. They were not merely executed; they were hacked to pieces and their murder shown on Syrian television. This precipitated the only act so far reported of any unit of the Israeli Army doing something on its own. Some of the fliers took off and flew over Damascus, located the television station, and bombed it out of existence.

# ✸ FIFTEEN

# A Yemenite Saga

FIFTY THOUSAND YEMENI were brought to Israel in Operation Magic Carpet, probably the most romantic chapter in the history of the great wave of immigration into Israel. These fifty thousand were flown seventeen hundred sixty miles in eight-hour nonstop flights in chartered American Skymasters.

The Yemeni say they have been in Yemen since the time of the destruction of Solomon's Temple—they were part of the Diaspora, the Dispersion. They lived and achieved and were comfortable, but after the Moslems conquered their land in the seventh century they sank into poverty, isolation, and degradation. The Jews in Yemen under the Moslems knew humiliation and the burden of special taxes. They had not only to pay the heavy regular taxes but also protection money to local Arab officials.

They were forbidden to wear colored robes and not permitted to ride a horse or a camel, but their spirit was not broken. The tenacity of the Jewish spirit was amazingly demonstrated through the more than a thousand years they dwelled in Yemen. Through all those centuries, the boys had been educated in Jewish religious schools, where they studied the Scriptures in Hebrew. They never gave up their belief that some day they would return to the Holy Land.

Though they had never seen a plane before they were flown into Israel, they were not astonished—had not the Lord said they would be brought to Israel on eagles' wings? One hundred forty were loaded on a plane (the average weight of the adults was only eighty-six pounds).

The Yemeni are easily distinguishable. They are slender, small-boned, not very tall. They have beautiful faces; some of the women have a cameolike beauty and lovely limpid eyes. They were the craftsmen of Yemen; they are gold- and silver-workers, jewelers, specialists in filigree work; they are potters and blacksmiths. It is difficult to believe, watching them as they integrate into the sophisticated life of modern Israel, that when they first arrived most of them had never slept in a bed, ridden in a train or bus, seen electric lights or piped water, or seen and used that most mundane but imperative appurtenance of civilization—a toilet.

For generations the Jews had relied on the words of Ezekiel: "Thus saith the Lord God, I will gather you from the people and assemble you out of the country where ye have been scattered and I will give you the land of Israel."

Long before Israel came into being as a nation, many Jews believing in this prophecy journeyed to this barren and inhospitable land. One of them was a Yemeni. He, his wife, their five children and a herd of sheep set out to walk from the hills of Yemen to the Holy Land. For six months they walked. They slept in tents, they bought food from the Bedouins, they endured heat by day, cold by night. They carried two of their children, fever raging through their small bodies, in their arms. Time came when the two little ones were no longer hot, but cold with the iciness of death. They knew hunger, they knew fear, but on they went, day after day, with the vision of the Holy Land and with God's promise, until —footsore, weary, and almost hopeless—they arrived at last in the Holy Land, where they could stop their endless and weary journey, for they had come home.

This Yemeni had been an artisan making gold ornaments in Yemen, but here he would till the soil, build a home, and make the land fruitful. His children increased in number, and their children also increased in number. One of these grandchildren married and had nine children. One of these nine, Yossie Levi, is principal of a high school in a suburb of Jerusalem. Yossie and four of his brothers fought in the 1967 war. So did their sister, who served in a communications center.

The family has been traditionally Orthodox. Yossie Levi wears a yarmulke, he will eat only kosher foods, and he observes the Sabbath faithfully. He won't work or ride on Saturday. There are no compromises in his Orthodoxy. He is a young man, about thirty-five, with fine chiseled features. He has an understanding nature, is intelligent and modern in his thinking, but observes the traditional conduct of the Orthodox Jew, untroubled by the question of what is the purpose of observing dietary laws that have no practical function in the twentieth century. He is a paratrooper. Before he was mobilized he and the children in the school of which he is principal dug shelters so that when the war came they could use the shelters for protection. After that he was ordered to join his unit.

As principal he was obliged to use his ingenuity when the first wave of immigrants entered Israel. Some parents would demand that their children be released from school so that they could help on the land. A number of times Levi solved this problem and managed to keep the youngsters in school by asking the whole class to go out and help the parents with their harvest so the son could continue in school. He told me of a Moroccan girl whose grades were so high that she received a scholarship, but the parents could see no point in her continuing school. She'd already gone to school; wasn't that enough? When she was sixteen they would arrange a marriage for her. What was the sense of more education for a girl? Ultimately they were persuaded to withdraw their objections, and the girl went on to one of the colleges. Now, of course, the parents beam with pride.

But these difficulties, he explained to me, took place only in the first five years when the immigrants arrived unfamiliar with the high priority the Israelis give to education. Now even the African Jews have accepted the mores of the Israelis and their standard of education for the girls as well as the boys.

Yossie Levi received his mobilization orders by radio. When he heard "Love of Zion," he knew he was being called to his unit. He hitch-hiked to his group, which was only half a mile from his home. Although a paratrooper, he can also handle a tank. As the men got into the tanks (they were on their way to Jerusalem), one of them said, "Hey, don't you think we ought to say a prayer?" Another said, "Fine, but what prayer?" (They obviously did not belong to the Orthodox group.) Whereupon Yossie handed them his keyring, on which was a printed prayer, which made the rounds of the tanks. It was certainly an unorthodox way of repeating a prayer, but Jerusalem fell to the Israelis.

"What about you, Yossie?" I said. "Weren't you afraid?" "Afraid of what?" he answered. "I knew I might be wounded; I knew I might even be killed; but I knew we would win."

"You knew you would win even with the whole Arab world against you, a hundred million of them, surrounded on all sides by enemies, with no country or nation at your side as an ally, and yet you were positive you would win? How come?"

"Well," he answered, "we were alone, it's true, and no other country did come to our aid, but you forget that we didn't need another country's aid; we had God on our side. Of course it was a miracle, but only God can perform a miracle and He wrought one."

"But," I persisted, "how did you know God would be on your side?"

He seemed amazed by my question. "But don't you know God promised we would live in the Holy Land, multiply, and prosper?"

"Oh, come on, Yossie," I said. "If God performed this miracle, he must also have been responsible for having allowed the gas chambers and the killing of six million Jews."

Yossie Levi looked at me sternly and answered me in words that are startling for a nonbeliever, as I am, but perfectly logical for a believer. He quoted the words of Ezekiel and said, "If the Jews of Germany had been good Jews, the concentration camps would not have happened."

"What do you mean?" I asked.

"Exactly what I said. If they had been good Jews, they would have left Germany, Russia, Poland, and all the other countries; they would have come to Israel as God commanded. Then they would have escaped the Nazis."

His logic left me stunned. Certainly I could not disprove his conviction, for it was too late now to know if the European Jews could have been saved. For Yossie Levi God is real; He is the national hero of the Jews and living in Israel is the result of the Covenant between the Jew and God. Therefore, since the Jew had come to the Holy Land, God would save it; God would protect it from the Arabs. This was obvious to him and those who believe as he does that the war was not really a contest—for the Jews were destined to conquer. It was merely a necessity to stop Arab attacks once and for all.

The angels certainly must have been spreading their wings over Israel during these days, because even when you have said that these are a brave group of men, that they are smart, even when you point out their superior education—even when you say all of these things, you wonder how they did it.

In forty-eight hours they had taken Jerusalem, conquered Jordan, Sinai, the Suez, the Gaza Strip. And in twelve more hours they were at the gates of Damascus, the Syrians having fled from the mountains. Their victories were so great they couldn't digest them. Their weapons were inferior in number and their equipment much less than that of the Arabs. They had suffered harassment for eighteen years; they had been shot at, they had endured an economic boycott, been denied the use of the Suez; they were more than two million people with a quarter-million Arabs living in their midst. They met an enemy equipped with better armaments and a battle cry sounded by King Hussein: "Kill, kill with your weapons, your hands, your arms, your teeth," as though he were a voice from the Middle Ages. Yet they were triumphant. Perhaps Yossie Levi was right. Perhaps it was a miracle wrought by God.

# SIXTEEN

# Egypt

NASSER, sounding more like a voice from the past than the head of a nation, roused Philip Toynbee to write to the *Times* of London: "President Nasser affirms the Arab intention is to massacre every Israeli, to enforce the exodus of the whole Israeli population. These aims are wicked, mad, and unsupportable."

On May 22, 1967, Nasser announced that under no circumstances would the Egyptians allow the Israeli flag to pass through the Gulf of Aqaba, and Radio Cairo—broadcasting for all Arabs—cried: "We pity you Jews; by God, we pity you! This will be our revenge for 1956."

On June 5, Ahmed Shukairy, head of the Palestine Liberation Organization (with an army of fifteen thousand trained for guerrilla warfare in Israel, armed with Russian and Red Chinese light weapons), announced: "We will wipe Israel off the face of the map and no Jew will remain alive."

On June 6, Radio Cairo claimed that Tel Aviv had been wiped out and that the Jews were flying across the desert. "We are drowning every Zion's coward in our hellfire. Now, Jews, you will see how your cowards die." Radio Cairo was either misinformed or just plain lying.

Nasser was cocky. He had four hundred planes and an antirocket unit with four missiles capable of penetrating the armor of any tank ever built. He had rapid-fire cannon, a new recoilless antitank gun, radar for controlling artillery fire on moving targets, an elaborate communications vehicle, and Russia's newest howitzer, which had a ten-mile range and was capable of firing five to seven rounds a minute. He also had Stalin tanks, which could theoretically cut the Israeli armor into bits.

Brigadier General Wafsi al Tall, commander of the Israeli Armored Corps, said later: "We are using old tanks, dating back to the Second World War. The enemy, both Egypt and Syria, had the most modern tanks. Egypt had brought seven divisions into Sinai against our three."

No wonder Nasser was cocky. He had the most modern armament in the world; he had the Arab countries with him, Russia as his ally and no other nation except Holland was willing to incur Arab enmity and help Israel. Even De Gaulle was on his side. Victory was to be his; how could he fail? But destiny was preparing to record an astonishing event, for on that fateful June day the sun rose on a sight perhaps never before witnessed by man. On that June morning with skies of brilliant orange and yellow, an Israeli plane took off every twenty seconds. All the radios were silent; they did not want Egypt to hear the communications between the fliers. The coordination was perfect. The pilots were seated in their planes, their watches synchronized; at twenty-second intervals they took off and in three hours had paralyzed twenty-five airfields. The Egyptian air force was totally destroyed. With the accuracy of birds winging to their nests, the Israeli pilots—husbanding their ammunition, ignoring the wooden dummies placed among the real planes—went unerringly to the Egyptian planes. Faster than the swallow flies they struck, and the blow for victory was delivered. The Arabs had thundered their boasts and the warning that no Israeli would be left alive, but it was the Israelis who struck like lightning. Thunder does not do the damage, it is the lightning that destroys and kills. There was never an air force like this! The Israeli fliers rocked the Arab bases with rockets—and with 30-mm. cannon fire when their bombs were gone. They flew with the speed of lightning, some even cracked the sound barrier; they let go their rockets with precision on the Russian jets lined up so obligingly for them. Not only did they destroy the air armada of the Arabs, given to them by the Russians, but as the Israeli pilots flew into the blue-and-golden sky that June morning, it was as though they had struck the nerve center of the Arabs and paralyzed it, for from that moment the Israeli chalked up one victory after another.

The Sinai victory was equally spectacular. It was unnerving flying over this desert afterward to see the tanks and planes, a graveyard of hardware, and the bodies of the Egyptians lying dead on the sands. One of the most moving sights was the number of shoes lying on the desert. Apparently the fleeing Egyptians took them off, because sand gets into a shoe and weighs it down, making walking difficult. The Israelis are not above using ordinary common sense. In one case they took so large a group of Arab prisoners they didn't have enough soldiers to guard them. So they ordered the Arabs to take off their belts. The reasoning was simple: how can a man run away with his pants falling down? If he holds his pants, he can't run fast; if he drops his pants, he's quite a sight. The big pile of belts after the Arabs removed them was not only an unusual sight but, if anything can be funny in a war, a funny one. But there was nothing funny to see flying over the Sinai Desert, for death among the Egyptians was monumental.

The Arab soldier had not been told by Cairo Radio that he as well as the Jews might be killed. The generally illiterate Arab soldier had been conscripted, was ignored by his officers, treated more like an animal than a human being, and the only motive instilled in him was hate. Sophisticated weapons were useless in his hands. The Israeli soldier didn't waste any energy hating. He was fighting for his existence.

# �֍ SEVENTEEN

# Jerusalem the Golden

I HAVE INTERVIEWED many mayors—from the Mayor of Taipei in Formosa to the Mayor of the city of Rome, but never had I interviewed a mayor who, on the day I talked with him, had had his city doubled in size and population. I walked into Mayor "Teddy" Kolleck's office with a formal letter of introduction. I never used it, for with an expansive gesture and cheery greeting he said, "What are you doing here?" He remembered that he had been a guest on my show in Cleveland.

"Oh," I answered, "I was in town and I thought I would drop in."

He grinned back. "Come up with me and I will show you my new Jerusalem."

"Well," he said. "How do you like my city?"

"I like it fine," I answered as I looked up at the sky and realized that Jacob, that Jesus, that Peter had looked up at the same sky; even Pontius Pilate had. Jerusalem is on the same latitude as Los Angeles, but because it is built on hills it is cooler and far less humid than Tel Aviv. I turned to the Mayor, with his boyish grin, and said, "What shall I tell them when I go back?"

"Tell them," he answered very quietly, "that we have come home."

Jerusalem the golden! What magic is there in these hills, these skies, these clouds, these buildings? The magic of dreams, of hopes, of history, and a mystical belief in destiny. In no way did the Mayor reveal the strain he must have been under. On the first day of the battle he visited every sector of the city to inspect the damage and to talk to the people. Once his driver hesitated to continue on because they had reached an open space that was under heavy fire.

"Never mind," the Mayor ordered, "if our time has come, it has come." A bullet cracked through the rear of his sedan, but he was unharmed.

Where the Mayor got his vitality I do not know. He had been in his office by seven that morning and would not leave until after midnight. The telephone kept ringing constantly, but everyone acted as if they had taken a dose of vitamins to give them extra strength so that each one could do what ordinarily would take four or five men to do. We descended the stairway and came back to the reception room and chatted with those gathered there waiting to talk to the Mayor. Someone brought in a tray with glasses of lemonade (there is very little alcoholic drinking in Israel, no drunkenness; tea is the universal drink). We drank a toast to the fall of Jordanian Jerusalem. They were all stunned by the quick victory. Suddenly the Mayor's city had doubled both in its population and in its problems.

As soon as Israel took the city it announced that people of all faiths, including the Arabs, would have access to its holy places, and that those places would be administered by representatives of both the Arabs and the Christians. What more could the Israelis have done? If they had proceeded as the Jordanians had when they held Jerusalem, the Arabs would have been excluded from that part of the Holy City. By comparison, the Israelis were generous.

The taking of Jerusalem was a bloody business of house-to-house fighting. Before the city fell a thousand Israeli homes had been pounded by mortar shells. I saw innumerable holes in the walls of many apartment houses. Amazingly enough, a week after the war, the city government was sending out repair men to replace windows or doors that had been shot out. I walked through the streets of Jerusalem and stopped to chat with a woman who was hanging out her wash. She shrugged her shoulders when I exclaimed about the wash. "So," she said, "should my family stay dirty because the Arabs have to have a war every ten years? Foo! I hope they all get headaches which should last them ten years."

I laughed at her vehemence and she smiled back. "Have you noticed," she added, "that the wind is breezier now that we have all of Jerusalem? Maybe my clothes will dry faster." What spirit those people have!

Mayor Kollek says he prefers not to speak of annexation but of the remarriage of the two halves of the city. The municipal services and the utilities have been unified. Jerusalem now has a single water, gas, electricity, garbage collection, postal, telephone, police, and school system. For the first time in history, the Old City has a twenty-four-hour-a-day water supply. The Old City is to be attached to the Israeli telephone system and will have direct-dialing service with the whole of Israel. Large quantities of foodstuffs have been shipped in. There are no shortages of anything, Kollek said.

There had been no compulsory schooling in the Old City under the former regime, and only about half the children attended school. "From September 1, schooling will be not only free but compulsory, as it is for all Israeli children. But Arab children will, of course, continue to be taught in their own language," the Mayor said.

Brigadier General Tchaim Herzog, Israel's military governor for occupied western Jordan, dissolved the former Arab city council the third day after Jerusalem fell and Kollek's city council took over. The Mayor said he might ask some of the former Arab councilmen to help, possibly setting up an Arab advisory committee.

Kollek noted that the preceding city council was elected by only about six thousand Arab voters out of a total population of seventy thousand. He said the Arab system gave the vote only to about twelve thousand males who pay property taxes, and about half of them voted.

However, in the next Jerusalem city elections, he said, the entire adult population of the Old City, men and women, will be entitled to vote for a new all-Jerusalem Council. Being under Israeli government may open new horizons and hope for the Arabs, and obviously if they have the vote they will elect their own representatives to the city council.

Perhaps never before has a people taken so much land, so many prisoners, so many cities that it could not digest its victories. Nothing in history can serve as a precedent, because nothing like this has ever happened before.

Israel will relinquish some of the land it holds, but only if the Arabs negotiate directly with the Jews. The

## Where Were the Arabs?

Israelis say the Arabs must recognize them—they must admit that Israel is a nation; that it exists and will continue to exist. "The Arabs must cease announcing that they will destroy us," one official told me. "We will not be destroyed; we propose to continue building our cities and cultivating our land. We have beaten you in a war which you started. We have no desire for war; it was the Arab nation who announced their intention to annihilate us. We have never threatened the Arabs; we are willing to live as neighbors. It is not reasonable, it is not sane or rational, to refuse to recognize Israel and to conduct themselves as though there were no Israel and yet wage war against us.

"Let the Arab nations sit down with us; let the Arab nations first admit that Israel is a fact and that Israel will continue as a nation. Then we will negotiate, and we will be reasonable."

It is absurd and is part of the fantastic Arab philosophy that the Israelis, who are the victors, are eager for peace and that the Arabs who are the vanquished sit sullenly plotting a renewal of the war.

And where else in recorded history has such an exchange of prisoners of war taken place as occurred on the Allenby Bridge in Jordan on June 27, 1967, when two Israeli fliers walked over the bridge in exchange for four hundred twenty-five Jordanian prisoners of war and three Iraqi consular officials? (In the 1956 Sinai campaign, five thousand Egyptians were returned for one Israeli prisoner of war.) Surely the Israelis have now won their right to their place in the sun.